Preparing *for* *Divorce* *while* *Happily* *Married*

TIPS FROM A DIVORCE LAWYER

JONATHAN J. FOGEL, ESQ.

Andover,
Minnesota

ISBN 13: 978-1-931945-45-5
ISBN 10: 1-931945-45-4

Library of Congress Catalog Number: 2005937836

Printed in the United States of America

First Printing: January 2006

10 09 08 07 06   5 4 3 2 1

Expert Publishing, Inc.
14314 Thrush Street NW,
Andover, MN 55304-3330
Andover,   1-877-755-4966
Minnesota   *www.expertpublishinginc.com*

To my wife, Robin,
who allowed me to write this book
without becoming too paranoid.

Contents

VII
The Great Custody Dispute, 51

VIII
Abuse, Abduction, and Accusations, 73

IX
Working with Experts, 83

X
Appropriate Behavior Once the Divorce has Started, 97

XI
Final Thoughts, 103

APPENDICIES

Acknowledgements

As usual, there are far too many people to acknowledge. However, I would like to specifically thank Mike Bresnahan, a great writer and even better friend. Without Mike's encouragement, I never would have organized the years of notes I had taken and put them into a book. I also want to acknowledge the contributions of Brian Bellmont. I want to thank all of the women at McFarland Cahill Communications. I want to thank M. Sue Wilson, an incredible attorney, a real mentor, and a true friend. I would also like to acknowledge Danny Fogel who posthumously inspired me to write a book. I want to thank my family for their never-ending support and encouragement. Finally, I want to thank my grandfather Henry Ginsburg. Without my grandfather's encouragement I never would have even applied to law school.

Preface

In 1997, I began keeping notes about all of the crazy things that happen during a divorce process; stories you can't make up even if you tried. I saved all those notes until one day in the summer of 2004, I realized these stories may have some beneficial purpose for others going through a divorce, thinking about getting divorced, or even happily married. I wanted to find a way to create a book that respected the sanctity of marriage while, at the same time, accepted the reality that over 50 percent of those marriages end in divorce.

I sat down and began writing. Whenever I finished a chapter, I would send it to my close friend Mike Bresnahan for unofficial editing. I really wanted to avoid the use of legalese so I assumed if he could understand the concepts of the book, I must be doing something right.

The original title of the book was *Planning for Divorce— While Happily Married.* After careful consideration, however, I decided to change "Planning" to "Preparing." I felt that "planning" is what you do for something that is inevitable. On the other hand, "preparing" is what you do for something that may come about, but you hope that it will not.

This book is not meant to be an exhaustive list of ways to prepare for a divorce. It is not meant to offend those individuals who have been through a very difficult and painful divorce process. I simply wanted to use real-life examples to show what the divorce process is like and how you can better be prepared if you are ever served with divorce papers or faced with the very tough decision of whether or not to file for divorce.

Introduction

There are a lot of books written about how to resolve marital disputes or how to amicably settle your divorce. This is not one of those books.

I have been representing clients in the area of family law for over ten years. During that time, I have handled hundreds of divorces, most of them involving the issue of custody. Every one of my clients started out the same, standing in front of friends and family, exchanging words of love and encouragement. Each one of them believed it would be "until death do us part…"

For some people in a crumbling marriage, though, death has begun to look like a pretty good alternative. Feelings change. People change. The reality is that almost one-half of those fresh-faced newlyweds will be divorced within seven years. I have often thought of how much easier my job would be, and how much cheaper it would be for my clients, if they had prepared for their divorce while they were still happily married.

Divorce can be a phenomenally costly process—both financially and emotionally. One wealthy client I worked with spent more than a half a million dollars on attorney's fees over a three-year period. But there are ways to reduce the costs of this high stakes game. There are ways to take control of the process. The type of preparation I discuss in this book can save you thousands of dollars in attorneys' fees—as well as many years of therapy.

The fact that you've picked up this book might mean you're just curious about what might happen if your thriving relationship takes an unexpected turn and breaks down in the future. Or, it might mean there's some little voice in the back of your head telling you something's not quite right. Maybe you and your spouse can work through it. I hope you do. But if you can't, and you're seriously starting to consider your options, this book could be a lifesaver.

I

The Death of a Dream

Getting a divorce is most often compared to a death in the family. In fact, statistics show that divorce ranks second only to the death of a child in terms of emotional turmoil, pain, and stress. In reality, a divorce is the death of a dream—a dream shared by two people hoping to create a life of happiness and fulfillment, a life where they would have children and grow old together. Unfortunately, when one, or both, of those individuals comes to the realization that their wonderful dream is over, life often becomes a nightmare.

Nobody marries with the expectation of failure. Married couples rarely contemplate that the person they just promised to love, honor, and obey might eventually become a stranger and perhaps even an enemy. Yet statistics paint an ugly picture. Approximately five out of ten first marriages today end in divorce. And the statistics for second marriages are even more grim.

When you buy a house, or a car, you don't expect your house will burn down, or you will be involved in an automobile accident totaling your vehicle. Nonetheless, you purchase the requisite amount of homeowner's or auto insurance to protect you in the case of an unanticipated catastrophe. Likewise, when two people get married, they don't anticipate a divorce. However, the likelihood of your house burning down, or being involved in a car accident, is far less than the chances of splitting with your spouse. I like to think of the information in this book as "divorce insurance."

As you will see from reading this book, if you wait until the divorce process has started to begin preparing for your divorce, it is too late; you will have already lost. The process of preparing for a divorce—or at least recognizing some of the important elements, and potential risks, procedures, and rules—must begin several years before the divorce has been initiated. For some people, that should mean starting to assess their situation as early as when they're sipping Mai Tais on the beach on their honeymoon—seriously. Preparing for a divorce involves lengthy and painstaking financial and professional commitments, and the sooner you begin to understand what could be at stake, the better.

If you do some research and take some of the precautions outlined in this book at the outset of your marriage, then stay happily married for the rest of your life, great. All you're out is some time and the cost of this book. But if you don't prepare and the "D-word" rears its ugly head down the road, you could pay for it for a long, long time.

High Stakes

Anyone who has been through an acrimonious divorce can tell you the dissolution process is a high stakes game—a game that requires strategic planning and pinpoint execution. Unfortunately for the players, they're not the ones controlling the board. It is often controlled by the judges, the experts, and most importantly, the attorneys. The soon-to-be-divorced couple is seemingly relegated to the status of pawns. Knowing the rules of the game can allow you to be a more proactive player and even come out on top.

Of course, divorce is not really a game. Far from it—divorce is a real-as-can-be experience that can have a deep impact on your life and the lives of your family. But as emotional as it can be, you need to start thinking about a divorce as a lawsuit, because that is exactly what divorce is. It is a lawsuit involving property, spousal maintenance, child support, and custody. Unlike other lawsuits, however, a jury does not decide a divorce case; a divorce proceeding is a "court trial." In other words, a judge decides your fate.

Now, just think about that for a moment: no jury of your peers, no suspenseful deliberation, no last-minute theatrics like those demonstrated by Matlock or Perry Mason. Real life divorce trials are very different from what you see on television or in the movies. In reality, a person wearing a black robe and wielding a gavel is given the power to decide the most important issues of your life: Who will have the custody of your children and how to divide the property you have worked your entire life to acquire. Don't you think your divorce is worth some preparation?

The key to a successful outcome, whether it's through a settlement or litigation, is preparation. The more prepared you are, the more likely you are to settle your case with a favorable outcome. Benjamin Franklin was correct when he said, "By failing to prepare, you are preparing to fail." If you can begin getting ready for the possibility of a divorce while you are still happily married, you will be in a much better position when, and if, the divorce process begins.

I don't condone underhanded tactics or dishonest behavior. That said, the first thing you will need to do after you purchase this book is find a good place to hide it. While it will likely become a valuable reference for you during the divorce process, the title may be somewhat offensive to your soon-to-be ex-spouse. More importantly, if you don't want your husband or wife to have access to this valuable information, I'd suggest keeping the book at your place of employment or in a safe deposit box.

Look at it this way: If you never use the information in this book, there's no need to worry your spouse by reading the book in his or her presence. And if you do move forward with divorce proceedings, it'll be to your advantage not to share the tips and techniques I discuss.

A Question of Control

One of the greatest contributors to divorce is the issue of "control"—either financial or personal. Who controls the bank account? Who sets the social agenda? When one partner to a marriage "controls," the other partner loses their sense of self. A divorce becomes imminent as the controlled partner tries to regain his or her self-esteem and decides they'd be better off without their spouse.

The issue of control is equally as important when you are going through the divorce process. In other words, the person who controls the process will generally end up receiving more of what they want.

Hopefully, as you read this book, you will find ways you can take control of your own divorce before it even starts.

II

Getting Started

Sometimes my clients are ready to start divorce proceedings the second they walk through my door. Something happened and they're prepared to dig in without another moment's hesitation. "Let's go!" they tell me. "I want to serve the papers right now, today."

But more often, clients are at the other end of the spectrum. Maybe they've just been served papers, and they were caught off guard. They now have a court deadline that says they need to respond within thirty days, and their minds are swirling with anger, fear, anxiety, and despair.

When they come into my office for the first time, I always say, out of habit, "It's nice to meet you," when really, it's not. It's a horrible situation in which to be introduced to someone. They might be sobbing uncontrollably. Or even if they're not, I can see them gripping the chair arm with such force I'm afraid their fingers are going to break. They're carrying a lot of emotion, and this may be the first time they've spoken to someone about what they're going through. They're often in an unfamiliar world, searching for a sense of understanding or reaching out for support.

I see my clients go through a whole range of emotions during the process. From grief to acceptance, different people go through different stages at different times, depending on a large and varied set of factors.

But one thing's for sure: There's a big difference between being the one who leaves versus the one who has been left.

The one who has been left often feels like it hit like a bomb, and when they walk in clutching their tissue, it's usually shock and disbelief. People are coming from really different places, and that's one of the tricks of guiding people through the process. It's seeing where they are, and then what needs to come next.

You may not even know where to begin. Maybe you know you need to leave your spouse, but you're finding it difficult to move forward. "How can I possibly get a divorce?" you might ask yourself. "I've been living with my husband since high school. He pays all the bills. He makes all the decisions. I don't know the first thing about being on my own." These concerns may seem antiquated, but more people are in this position at the time of their divorce than you may think.

It's a common refrain. But one, I'm happy to say, that can be overcome. The first thing I try to do is to get my clients talking. I ask, "Why don't you tell me why you're here and what you think I can help you with?" With that little bit of prompting, I'm often amazed at how much they'll start to tell me—someone they've never met before. Once that faucet turns on, they'll release a deluge of emotion and fact, "He did this," or "She did that." And I'm scrambling to take notes.

We then talk about what we can do. Where do they want to go from here? Do they need an Order for Protection right away because of abuse? Maybe they've been served with divorce papers and we need to file an answer. Or maybe we look into filing a petition and get the divorce proceedings started.

Sometimes they want to get started slowly, with mediation. They're not ready to file for divorce, but they know the marriage is over, and they don't want to spend the cost on court right away. They might want to begin negotiations with their spouse. If that's the case, I write a letter to the opposing party saying something like this, "I've been retained by your wife (or husband). We don't want to start litigation, but my client feels the marriage is over. If you have an attorney, please forward this letter to them. Otherwise, please call me and we can talk about possibly setting up mediation."

I try to start out with the least aggressive approach. I can always be more forceful. I've found that if I start out too aggressively, it's difficult to pull back. Once the proverbial genie's out of the bottle, it's hard to cram it back in.

It Takes a Village

Divorce is probably the most emotional type of litigation. You're not selling someone a building or negotiating a contract. You aren't keeping an arm's-length business detachment. This is your life we're talking about here.

Most of the people who come through our offices have never gone through a divorce before, and many will probably never go through one again. Most of them have never even imagined they'd be dealing with a divorce. It's destroying their dream of living together happily ever after. The fairy tale is turning ugly.

Traditionally, women in divorce proceedings are the ones who lose financially. Their standard of living may drop as much as 30 percent in the first year following a divorce. I've had wives stare at me almost catatonically while I talk. They are lost in a world of uncertainty and dread. Men may not suffer as greatly financially, but they tend to lose precious time with their kids. I've had husbands break down in my office, saying, "Why is she going for sole physical custody? I'm a good dad; she's accusing me of being a bad father."

One of the things I try to do is help my clients find resources outside my legal counsel. I call this my "team" approach to handling a divorce. Does my client need a financial planner? A therapist? A Realtor? A hug? Getting a divorce is a very difficult thing, and clients often need someone else to talk to. Legally, I can help. But emotionally, psychologically, there are people better suited to help than I am.

When people are going through a divorce and hammering out what the legal agreements are going to be, or even the financial agreements, they're called upon to do pretty high-order thinking. A lot of decision-making that goes on during a divorce process has long-term ramifications. This type of high-order thinking is supposed to take place at a time when clients are maybe the most stressed they've ever been.

I worked with a client whose husband was having an affair—and abusing his wife. For their entire marriage, he was the one who was in control of the finances. The woman came in; she was an absolute wreck, barely able to keep it together. Because she was so preoccupied with the emotional and practical aspects of the huge change she was about to make, she could barely concentrate on the legal aspects of her impending divorce. We talked a while about how overwhelmed she felt, and I referred her to a therapist and a financial planner I trusted.

A few weeks later, I met with her again. This time she appeared to be a totally different person, beaming with anticipation. "I met with the financial planner and the therapist, and they both told me I can do this," she said, smiling. "We talked about the feelings I'm going through. We talked about where I can put my money. But here's the best part—we made a budget, and I'll be able to make it on my salary."

Her anxiety over whether she would be able to survive without her husband's financial support was all encompassing. But her conversations with the therapist and financial planner–two experts who knew the right questions to ask and the right things to tell her–helped her let go of her fears.

She was extremely grateful for the referrals, but really, all I did was put her in touch with talented people I thought could help her. A lot of attorneys don't even go that far, though. They don't let themselves get emotionally invested in their clients, not even a tiny bit. They bill hour after hour, with one thought on their minds: "I'll get her through her divorce, then move on to the next client."

I think that's a mistake, and I think it's bad business. By ignoring the issues people are going through outside of the courtroom, you never really deal with the issues that are coloring their decisions—decisions that can affect every legal move you make. By helping my clients get a handle on their stress and emotions, our collaboration is much more fruitful. By addressing and working through the animosity, anger, fear, or frustration, they're able to focus on the larger picture. We're both able to concentrate on making the very best legal decisions. The clients are able to focus on what's in their best interests and not be bogged down with unresolved feelings.

I once represented the wife in a dissolution matter where she and her husband were contemplating bankruptcy just as they were beginning their divorce proceedings. She was beside herself with fear. I sat her down with a financial planner who told her she could indeed not only survive on her own, but actually thrive. I work with a lot of clients who have never dealt with the finances in their households, and who may not even have the slightest inkling how much money they have—or where it is.

Typically, in a marriage, there's going to be one person who tends to be stronger in the finances. I see one of my jobs as educating the clients, providing information to them so they have as much knowledge as possible, so when they speak with their spouse about how to split up the assets, they feel they're on a level playing field.

Matching clients with a competent financial planner, not only puts them at ease, I find we can often use the information in our legal work, too. The detailed financial data they put together–whether budgeting information or projected income–can often be used as exhibits in court.

Or it helps in our discussions designed to figure out how much spousal maintenance my clients really need to survive. They might want two thousand dollars a month, but based on the budget they put together with the financial expert, it's obvious they could get by with $1,500. Often, when they see the numbers on paper in the form of a budget (and also realize that it may cost them an additional thirty thousand dollars in attorney's fees to pursue the extra cash), they decide to settle.

Family Law 101

Family law is an interesting genre of law. Ninety-nine percent of other attorneys' faces pucker when they think about family law. "How do you guys deal with all that stuff?" they ask. "Doesn't it make you cynical? Doesn't it make you depressed?"

The answer, for me anyway, is yes, sometimes it can be tough. But more often, it's extremely rewarding. Obtaining a million-dollar settlement for a client whose damaged self-esteem never let her think she would be entitled to anything; helping a gay man win custody of his son from his ex-wife, a poor parent; or helping a client reunite with her daughter after her ex-husband fled with the child out of state—it's a gratifying job. Drafting a contract for the sale of a company doesn't compare to the feeling you get when you reunite a mother with her child or negotiate the best possible property settlement for a grateful client.

It is important to note that not all states handle divorce in the same way. The grounds for divorce depend on the state, and may be based on "no-fault" or "fault." A no-fault divorce is available in some form in all fifty states; many states also have fault-based grounds as an additional option. A no-fault divorce is one in which neither the husband nor the wife officially blames the other for the breakdown of the marriage. Common basis for no-fault divorce are "irreconcilable differences," "irretrievable breakdown," or "incompatibility." Another common basis for no-fault divorce is that the parties have lived separately for a certain period of time (this varies from state to state) with the intent that the separation be permanent.

The list of grounds for a fault-based divorce may include: adultery, physical cruelty, mental cruelty, attempted murder, desertion, habitual drunkenness, use of addictive drugs, insanity, impotency, and infection of one's spouse with venereal disease. I've included a table in Appendix A that summarizes the law in each of the fifty states as it relates to "fault" versus "no-fault" divorce and residency requirements.

A lot of attorneys–especially new attorneys–think they can just pick up a divorce file and handle it. "Oh, it's just a divorce. How hard is that?" they'll say. "I'll take on divorce cases if business gets slow." The reality is a divorce case deals with so many areas: tax, real estate, custody, property division, preserving assets, tracing non-marital assets. I sometimes think a lot of people perceive family law as simply splitting the assets. "Okay, let's just cut everything in half. Who wants the house?"

Even my clients' perceptions are a little off when they first come in. We sit down and start to discuss their situation, and they tell me, "I think it's really amicable. We've talked about it."

"Okay," I'll answer. "What have you discussed about custody?"

They'll think for a minute, then say, "Well, we haven't really talked about that, but I don't think it'll be a problem."

And then the red flag goes up in my head. A husband comes in and says, "Yeah, I'm pretty sure she'll agree to joint physical custody." But when I explain that would mean she would get less child support, and maybe her attorney is encouraging her to ask for full custody, his confident expression turns to concern. A lot of people think it'll be a breeze, but it can be extremely complicated.

If you choose the right attorney, however, it'll be a whole lot easier.

III

How to Pick, or Eliminate, a Divorce Attorney

It is extremely important to hire a good lawyer early in your divorce planning process, possibly even before you've made a final decision about ending your marriage. Think that sounds premature? Not at all.

We all consult experts about almost every aspect of our lives. We visit a doctor to get an idea of whether we're healthy or not. We go to an accountant at the beginning of the year to discuss what we might do to reduce our tax liability for the next twelve months. We sit down with an estate-planning attorney to make plans for our assets after we eventually pass away. A divorce attorney is no different. He or she is an expert in clearing a path through the often dangerous jungle of family law, custody, and asset retention.

Consulting with a divorce attorney before you actually need one is a great way to learn about what to expect during the divorce process, and to help you avoid mistakes that could later cost you dearly.

There are many lawyers to choose from, so it's important you ask pertinent and important questions in order to pick an attorney that is knowledgeable and right for you.

Choosing an Attorney

I have provided a list of obvious, as well as not-so-obvious, questions for you to ask. Be sure to bring a list of prepared questions with you to your initial visit so none of them slip your mind. In addition, bring a pen and paper so you can take notes. You will probably not remember most of what is said during that meeting; it's often a very emotional hour.

Remember, your attorney person is going to be the link between you and your future relationship with your children, as well as your assets, so spend some time selecting the attorney that is right for you.

Begin contributing to a divorce fund early. I suggest that immediately following your return from the honeymoon, you create a separate divorce fund. For example, open a savings account at a bank in which you and your spouse don't have any existing accounts. During the course of your marriage, make small deposits into this account on a regular basis, either monthly, quarterly, or annually, whichever you feel is best. The key is to make the deposits small enough so your spouse doesn't notice the money is missing.

By the time you are ready to file for divorce, the divorce fund should give you a sufficient amount to cover any retainer requested by your attorney, generally in the range of $5,000 to $10,000, and may be even enough to pay your entire attorney's fees, if the account was earning a decent amount of interest. This divorce fund will have to be disclosed as an asset during the divorce process, but remember, you don't want to be the spouse who is unable to hire the best divorce lawyer because you don't have access to enough funds.

If you never get a divorce, use the money in your divorce fund to take your spouse on a wonderful trip for your fiftieth wedding anniversary.

Obvious Questions

Ask about the attorney's experience in family practice, and specifically divorce. You don't want to hire someone who is just starting out in the practice of family law. There are many intricacies and "tricks" and nuances that can only be learned with experience. Now is not the time to give the rookie a chance to get into the game.

Ask the attorney to explain the legal issues as well as the legal process in your particular county. Your attorney should be able to very easily explain to you the general concepts and legal issues involved in your case. You are not going to want to hire an attorney who needs to refer back to the statute book every time you—or the judge—has a question.

Ask how much the attorney will charge per hour or increments of the hour. Some attorneys have different rates for in-court time versus out-of-court time. You will want to know that up front. In addition, be sure to ask how the attorney bills for incremental time periods. Some attorneys break down their time into tenths of an hour, while other attorneys will charge a minimum for drafting a letter or appearing in court.

Ask how much the attorney expects it will cost. Do not, however, expect the attorney to give you a specific quote on fees. Generally, the attorney will give you a rough estimate of total charges and a list of services covered by that estimate. The more experienced lawyers should be able to give you a roadmap of the process and how much each step will cost. You should be very skeptical about an attorney who quotes you a fixed rate or guarantees that your entire divorce will only cost a specific amount. Remember, you get what you pay for.

Ask about their experience with the opposing attorney, if there is one already involved. It is very helpful to know that your attorney has dealt with opposing counsel in the past. You will want your attorney to know the opposing counsel's weaknesses, preferences, and tendencies. A lot of times, your attorney can tell you how the case might proceed, depending who is representing your soon-to-be ex-spouse.

Not-So-Obvious Questions

How much of the work will be done by paralegals and/or younger associates? Generally speaking, most attorneys will work with a paralegal who is responsible for a lot of the day-to-day workings of the file. The nice thing about having a paralegal work on your case is they typically charge significantly less per hour than an attorney. It is important to know this up front.

What is the attorney's strategy or game plan to obtain the results you are looking for? Your attorney should be prepared to provide you with an overall strategy. This will assure that your attorney will be proactive and not just reactive, which will save you time and money in the long run. Remember, the strategy may change during the course of the proceeding, but the overall goals should remain the same.

Has the attorney ever been subject to discipline by the Board of Professional Responsibility? Do not be afraid to ask your potential attorney this question. If the answer is yes, you are going to want all of the details before hiring this individual. You might not want to rule out an attorney just because he or she has been disciplined, but it's a red flag that needs to be scrutinized. There are several different levels of discipline—anywhere from private wristslapping to suspension to disbarment—and each says different things about the attorney. What type of discipline did the attorney receive?

Just remember to take any complaint you hear about the attorney with a grain of salt. Divorce is such an emotional process that clients are far more likely to lodge a complaint than with other areas of the law. In fact, family law attorneys have the highest incidence of complaints registered against them as compared to all other areas of practice.

Will I receive a copy of all correspondence concerning my case? The rules of most state bars require regular communication with the client, which includes, but is not limited to, receiving copies of all correspondence. Personally, I make it a practice to send to the clients a copy of every piece of paper that comes in or goes out of my office dealing with their case. That way, the clients always know what's going on and can keep their own file at home.

Other tips for finding and working with the right attorney

Find out if the lawyer has credibility with the judges in your particular county. It's important to hire a lawyer who is respected by the judges. A judge, not a jury, is the one who needs to ultimately make decisions about your divorce, and if he or she believes your attorney isn't being straightforward, that's going to negatively affect your case. Ask around. If other people are labeling an attorney as dishonest, there's no doubt the judges are chatting about him or her as well. Judges, like anybody else, talk to each other. They may go to each other for advice, or they may compare notes about attorneys, especially rotten ones. In fact, my first job after law school was clerking for a District Court Judge, and I saw the judges actually comparing horror stories about incompetent attorneys.

Ask friends for references. Statistics show that at least one person you know has had to use the services of a divorce attorney. Ask that person what they thought of their lawyer. Most people find their own attorney using this approach. In fact, almost all of my clients now come to me from the referral of a past client or an acquaintance of that client. These people will be able to give you first-hand knowledge of the attorney's strengths and weaknesses. They can tell you if the attorney promptly returns phone calls and makes themselves available when you need them.

Contact the Bar Association. In order to practice law, all attorneys must pass the Bar exam in the state in which they are practicing with a few exceptions. Once admitted to practice, most attorneys will join a local, state, or national bar association. These organizations can be a great resource for finding a divorce attorney. Most of these organizations will have a toll free number. The American Bar Association, which is located at 321 North Clark Street, Chicago, IL 60610, can be reached at 1-800-285-2221, or on the Internet at www.abanet.org. You can also contact your local or state bar association. When doing so, you can ask for a list of certified specialists in the area of family law, if your state has such a designation.

Use the Internet. Most attorneys today have a web site or at least a presence on the Internet. You can simply run a web search for family law attorneys in your area. You can also visit www.martindale.com, a legal network that contains a database of more than one million lawyers and law firms in 160 countries.

Hire the most experienced attorney you can afford. Don't make the mistake of thinking that the hourly rate of an attorney is an indication of how expensive your divorce will be. In fact, an attorney who charges a higher rate may be more well-versed in the areas of alternative dispute resolution and more efficient than a less expensive attorney. In addition, the work product of a more experienced attorney will certainly be more detailed and better protect your interests.

Pay attention to the bill. Other attorneys might not like what I'm going to say, but don't be afraid to question the bill from the attorney. It's your prerogative as the client. You are probably being charged a lot of money for the services being provided, so you should take the time to review every billing statement you receive in order to ensure it is accurate and appropriate.

"You're Fired!" If you are unhappy with the services being provided by your attorney, if your attorney is failing to return your phone calls, or if you no longer have confidence in your attorney's abilities, fire them. Remember, you are the client and you are no doubt paying a lot of money for your attorney's services; make sure you are getting what you deserve.

Trust your gut. In the end, it will probably boil down to your own gut feeling about the attorney. Trust that feeling. If you spend the entire meeting wondering why your stomach is churning and you can't get the bad taste out of your mouth, you should probably look elsewhere. On the other hand, if you leave the meeting with a sense of trust and the feeling that your questions have been answered, I suggest you stick with that attorney.

Eliminating Attorneys

While it is important to find a good attorney for yourself, it is equally as important that you make sure your soon-to-be ex-spouse does not have an opportunity to hire the best attorney in town. In order to accomplish this goal, you will need to be prepared to do some legwork and possibly spend some money in the process. This is what people in the legal industry call "conflicting out an attorney," and it happens a lot more often than you think. Here's how it works:

Creating Ethical Conflicts. Don't concern yourself with the five best attorneys in your geographical area; it is the attorneys who have a reputation as being the biggest jerks that will cost you the most financially and emotionally if they are representing your soon-to-be ex-spouse. In order to find out who these five attorneys are, just ask around; I guarantee that many people will know them by name.

Make an appointment to see each one of them separately. Generally, each attorney will charge an initial consultation fee. This will range anywhere from $150 to $350 dollars, depending on the attorney's hourly rate. Believe me, this will be the best money you ever spend.

You'll want to pay for this initial consultation either with cash or with money from an account that only you monitor. The last thing you want is to have your spouse see the law firm of "Dewey, Cheatham, and Howe" show up on the credit card bill or the check register—before he or she has an inkling that you may be considering a divorce.

The meetings will usually last for approximately one hour—the longer the better. During that meeting, you'll want to give the attorney as much intimate knowledge about your case as possible, including details about your finances, and any infidelities, drug addictions, or other skeletons in your closet you probably never thought you'd talk about. The more intimate the details shared during this meeting, the more likely it will be that the attorney will not be able to represent your spouse during your divorce, and that is the ultimate goal. Remember, you don't have to hire the attorney in order to create a conflict. You've just got to make it through the initial meeting.

By giving each attorney intimate details about you and your marriage, you are creating an attorney-client relationship. Once that is established, that attorney is prohibited from representing someone whose interest may be contradictory to your own, and that includes your soon-to-be ex-spouse.

If your spouse then calls one of these attorneys for possible representation, the attorney's office will run a "conflicts check," checking their database of current and former clients, or potential business or personal conflicts. (Despite what many people think, attorneys are actually bound by certain rules of professional responsibility and ethics.) This procedure is done for the purpose of determining whether or not the attorney has ever represented, or consulted with, someone with adverse interests.

And if you've already established an attorney-client relationship with many of the top lawyers in town, then your spouse is out of luck. He or she will learn the bad news that their dream attorney has already met with you and is therefore precluded from signing on as their lawyer.

Sneaky? Maybe. Essential? Absolutely. It's a commonly accepted tactic. And you might want to consider giving it a try, because while you're reading this, your soon-to-be ex-spouse might already be sitting in your dream attorney's office.

IV

Weighing Your Options– Alternative Dispute Resolution

You might have an image of how divorce is often portrayed on TV-two sharply dressed teams of attorneys presenting compelling arguments in front of a curmudgeonly judge. But litigation–using the courts to come to an agreement–is by no means the only option for solving a dispute.

Alternative Dispute Resolution (ADR) is gaining in popularity in states from coast to coast. It's exactly what you might guess: An alternative to litigation as a way to resolve contentious issues between the parties.

Almost every state has a law that requires the use of some form of ADR, unless there has been domestic abuse between the parties. In fact, some states will not allow the parties to come to court until they have exhausted all of their ADR options. In most states, it used to be that this requirement only applied to civil litigation. However, the state legislatures recognized the need to cut back on the amount of litigated divorce cases.

Some counties stand out above the rest as leading the way to make the divorce process less acrimonious. In Minnesota's Hennepin County, for instance, they're trying model programs that are being implemented across the country, including what's called Early Neutral Evaluation. Research shows that the faster a case gets to an evaluator or mediator the more likely the case will be resolved. The parties involved are less likely to make nasty accusations about their spouse and bog down the proceedings with finger-pointing and blame. The counties try to move these cases through quickly to put pressure on the parties to settle.

Depending upon the jurisdiction you live in, there are several alternatives to litigation to choose from. If handled appropriately, these options can prove to be less expensive financially–and emotionally–than a trial.

Generally speaking, the ADR options are as follows:

Arbitration. This is a process in which a third party, selected by the husband and wife, or their attorneys, is given the authority to make a binding decision on the issues presented. This can include a wide variety of topics, from spousal maintenance and custody to property division and child support. The arbitrator acts in much the same way as a judge would. He or she is paid by the divorcing couple, and the cost will vary greatly depending on the expertise of the arbitrator.

The benefit to using an arbitrator is that the proceedings will generally take less time and are far less formal than a court trial. The downside is that if you are unhappy with the decision, you may be limited on your appeal options and you will have wasted quite a bit of financial resources attempting to settle.

Mediation. This is a very informal dispute resolution process in which a neutral third party attempts to help the parties reach an agreement. The role of the mediator is not to make binding decisions, but to assist the parties in resolving conflicts. The mediator is not there to pick sides or give legal advice.

One of the chief benefits of mediation is that it is much cheaper than arbitration or going to court. (On the other hand, if the other side has no intention of settling, you might just be wasting your time and money by going to mediation.)

Some states or counties offer a free, or very inexpensive, mediation program. The parties, however, are always allowed to hire their own private mediator, if they have the funds to do so. Generally speaking, a private mediator will ask for a retainer at the outset; the amount will depend on their level of expertise. You can expect to pay between $5,000 and $7,500 for an experienced mediator.

Mediation creates an environment in which people can safely explore various options and come up with agreements or solutions to what is facing them and their family. Anything that is said or discussed during the mediation process is inadmissible in court. This rule about confidentiality fosters an open and honest forum for everyone involved without the fear of having their offers of settlement used against them on the witness stand.

Collaborative Law. This is a fast-growing approach to handling divorce cases, as well as other litigation. In this process, the parties agree at the beginning that they will reach a settlement without going to court. This process is much less formal than regular litigation. There's no formal discovery, and if the parties are unable to reach an agreement, and either party wishes to litigate, both parties must fire their lawyers and hire new counsel—in effect starting over from scratch. This creates a huge incentive to settle.

The upside to this process is that it generally avoids the need for those "he said, she said" affidavits, filled with name-calling and slanderous statements. On the other hand, the downside is you will have spent quite a bit of time developing a working relationship with an attorney whom you will have to fire if you are unable to settle.

Attorneys and ADR

While I support the idea of ADR, I believe it is absolutely necessary that you be represented by an attorney before, during, and after that process. It is very important to remember that the mediator, arbitrator, or whatever neutral decision-maker you select, is not there to advocate for you or look out for your best interest. The ADR neutral's only objective is to facilitate a settlement; they are generally not allowed to provide any legal advice, even if they are a licensed attorney.

These alternatives to litigation work best when both parties are willing to come to the table with the intention of compromising. It is also very important that both parties are on a level playing field throughout the process. Therefore, you should be sure to come to the ADR session fully aware of your bottom line and leave your resentment at the door.

There's a lot to be gained by sitting back and listening to what the other side has to say during ADR discussions. As I stated earlier, nothing said during the ADR process can be used if the divorce goes to trial later on. (Otherwise, it wouldn't promote the open and honest discussion the system is encouraging.) But a lot of times things do come up during mediation that a good attorney will take note of, and use to gauge their case's strengths and weaknesses, or use as a negotiating tool down the road.

Prior to ADR, you should work very closely with your attorney in order to adequately prepare. Your attorney should provide you with an idea of what will happen during the ADR process and should be available during the process if you have any questions, legal or otherwise. Once again, the key to a successful ADR process is preparation.

Negotiation

One thing to keep in mind is a very small percentage of divorce cases actually make it to trial. In fact, most cases settle at some point before ever making it in front of a judge. I always tell clients at the beginning there are two paths we can go down: litigation or negotiation. Litigation, by its very structure, leaves little room for negotiation. Once you're in front of a judge, he is limited by what the law says and what it allows him or her to do.

On the other hand, if we go down the path of negotiation (which includes mediation and other forms of Alternative Dispute Resolution), we can be very creative. Judges tend to enforce just about anything the two parties agree to, as long as it doesn't put the children at risk.

A client told me she wanted her husband to pay their children's college expenses. I told her the law couldn't force him to do that—once a child turns eighteen, parental support can't be mandated by the court. We decided to negotiate.

And to do that well, we needed to make sure we were on the same page. So I gave my client a pile of information on what the law says regarding spousal maintenance and child support. I asked her to read the statute carefully. She did, and she told me she had a much better understanding of what her position could be on the issue. She felt empowered.

Then, we looked at contingencies. We talked about what to do if the other side came back with a counter-offer. We talked about, "If this happens, then we do this. If that happens, then we do that." Of course, we could sit there all day and deal with what ifs, so we didn't linger on them, and only tackled the most important ones up front.

Armed with her newfound confidence based on her knowledge of the statute, we entered into negotiation with her ex-husband. He eventually agreed to pay for college expenses, and now—even though the court couldn't order it—it is enforceable.

Use of Experts in ADR

When outside experts are hired as neutrals during an ADR process, it can help facilitate the entire experience.

It's common for financial planners to be hired in a neutral capacity. In that situation, they are helping clients to pull together their balance sheet and work through their cash flow numbers.

The beauty of ADR is that things are usually more transparent. There's not a lot of game playing. With a typical divorce, you use position-based negotiation, where one party will throw out their, 'I want the house, I want the 401K, and I want $5,000 in maintenance a month.' Then the other side will throw out, 'No, I want the house, and I'm not paying any maintenance.' You don't necessarily know what's really important to the other side. They're just asking for the world because they know they're going to have to compromise.

But most ADR is interest-based. With interest-based negotiations, you're just trying to find out what the priorities are for each person.

Some experts say acting as a neutral party in a collaborative law proceeding allows them to subscribe to the old phrase from *Dragnet* TV series, "Just the facts, ma'am."

Most neutral experts will tell the clients that they are not a hired gun. That's what your attorney is for. Your attorney is your personal advocate.

Other experts, like business valuators agree that being able to focus on the facts–rather than getting caught up in the emotions of a case–can really make things easier. By being completely professional and getting people to trust them, or at least trust what they are doing as part of the case, I think that just helps. It doesn't always work. Sometimes there's just way too much animosity in the case. But when it does work, it's kind of a nice feeling to know that maybe you helped it get done cheaper, more amicably, and helped people get on with their lives.

But working with a neutral expert comes with its own set of challenges. They sometimes have *nobody* telling them the truth. The husband, if he owns the business, is telling me how bad business is. The wife is saying, 'Well, he told me it was worth $10 million.' So you've got those issues going on, trying to filter to the truth.

I think it's a disservice to the process and the neutral experts if the clients are not fair, open, and honest with someone that's trying to figure out what your assets are worth. Neutral experts should try to remain as independent and objective as possible, but if they think someone's lying to them, they need to go that much further just to try and figure out the truth.

I'll admit that our legal system is imperfect. But even though it's flawed, it has the potential to give both parties what they need, and sometimes even what they want.

To benefit from the system, though, you have to be prepared. And if you pay attention to the tips I'm about to discuss, you will be.

V

Timing Your Divorce

Okay, you've decided you've finally had enough. Going back to the issue of control, if you feel as if your spouse is about to file for divorce, you'll gain a bit of power by being the one to actually do the serving. The most important element you can control? Timing.

The timing of your divorce may carry with it a significant financial impact. For example, in a single-income family, the non-working spouse may not have earned enough money to qualify for Social Security at the age of retirement. However, if spouses are married at least ten years and don't remarry, the non-earning spouse may qualify for Social Security benefits based on the ex-husband's or ex-wife's earnings when both reach the age of sixty-two. If you're the non-earning spouse, you may want to hang in there to make it to your tenth wedding anniversary.

And that's just one element to take into consideration. Here's how timing can minimize the financial burden of getting divorced:

Wait until you have a terrible year financially.

You should pick a year you believe will be your worst financial year. In other words, don't wait until you have that one breakthrough year financially to file for your divorce. Remember, the court will determine your child support and spousal maintenance obligation based upon your current income, so be sure to strike while the iron is hot, or cold, depending on how you look at it.

In fact, if you ever wanted to quit your job and start your own business, this is the time to do it. If you wait until the divorce process has been initiated, the court is allowed to assign an income to you based upon your earnings history. The longer you are self-employed, the harder it becomes for the court to determine your income.

Wait until your spouse is gainfully employed or going back to school.

Encourage your stay-at-home husband or wife to get a part-time job. A position where he or she works even just a few hours a week can go a long way toward offsetting your obligation for spousal support. In the eyes of the court, the next best thing to gainful employment is to be working toward a degree. So if your husband or wife always wanted to go back to school, now would be a great time to encourage them to follow their dream.

Think about your living arrangements.

The first option is to remain in the family home. However, if you believe this will not be an option, you want to make sure you have alternate living arrangements prior to filing for divorce, especially if you have minor children. If possible, try to find a place within the same school district as your kids. This will increase your chances of being awarded joint, or even sole, physical custody.

Protect your stuff before you file for divorce.

Be sure to remove any items of personal property–at least those you want to see again–from the home prior to filing for divorce. It is not uncommon for items of sentimental value to mysteriously disappear once the Summons and Petition are served upon the soon-to-be ex-spouse. You will need to itemize every piece of property you remove from the home. However it is better to have those items in your safe possession.

I once ended up with a case where a husband decided he was going to have his wife served with the Summons and Petition while he was at work so he wouldn't have to be at home when she got the news. My client told me he waited the entire day to receive that telephone call from his wife, telling him how sorry she was and that she would do anything to get him back. Finally, at 6:30 p.m. he couldn't wait any longer and he had to go home to face his wife and pack his things. When my client opened the front door he was shocked to find a completely empty house, except for one piece of paper taped to the refrigerator, which contained four words, "See you in court." By the end of the case, I was able to retrieve 99 percent of his personal belongings, but it cost him thousands of dollars, all of which could have been avoided with just a moment of preplanning.

VI

The Honeymoon's Over: Preserving your Personal Property and Other Assets

To get the most out of preparing for a potential divorce, the earlier you start laying the groundwork, the better. Some of these tactics may seem extreme, but believe me, they're necessary.

Again, my main goal with this book is to tell you how to protect yourself in the event of a divorce. And as unsavory as some of these ideas might seem to you, particularly if you're only reading this as a "what if" scenario and not actively planning to leave your spouse, each is designed to give you that difficult-to-obtain advantage in a divorce—control.

Even if you decide not to put some of these ideas into effect, at least pay attention to the rationale behind my advice.

Oops, I forgot the pre-nup. A prenuptial agreement (or pre-nup) is an efficient and commonly used way to protect your assets. Simply, a pre-nup is an agreement between two people who are going to get married that outlines who will get what in the event of a divorce.

But what happens if your marriage is falling apart, and you neglected to sign a pre-nup before you walked down the aisle? Well, in some states, a new option is starting to emerge—what's called a "post-nup." That's right. Believe it or not, if you can convince your spouse to sign a post-nuptial agreement, you might still be able to protect your assets. This is a relatively new phenomenon, so make sure to check with an attorney in your area to see if your state recognizes post-nups, and to make sure you're following all the local rules.

A brief word of warning: If you do plan to ask your husband or wife for a post-nup, you'd better be good and ready to get a divorce, because a request like that usually doesn't go over too well.

Keep the wedding list and gift list; you never know when they might come in handy. I handled a case where the parties, despite their best efforts, stayed married for only sixteen months. My client, luckily, kept the list that the parties had created on their computer for writing thank you notes to their wedding guests. This proved to be very useful when it came to dividing personal property. We used the list to determine which relative gave which gift, and we then simply agreed to award each item of personal property to the person whose closest relative gave the gift.

In other words, if the husband's Aunt Sally gave the happy couple a bread maker as a wedding gift, it would be awarded to him. On the other hand, if the wife's third cousin, twice removed, gave them a crystal candy dish, it would be awarded to her. This exercise probably saved my client–and his ex-wife–$5,000 to $10,000 in attorney's fees.

Keep debts in your spouse's name and assets in your name. When it comes to credit cards, it is okay to have a "companion" card, but try to keep the account in your spouse's name only. Although most states consider all debts incurred during the marriage to be marital, and therefore subject to division, it is better to keep debts out of your name.

For example, let's say the wife opens a Bloomingdale's credit account. She proceeds to charge more than $10,000 worth of designer clothes. The marriage falls apart. At the time of the divorce, the court has the authority to order the husband to pay the outstanding balance on the credit card. However, Bloomingdale's is not bound by the court's decision. In other words, if the husband refuses to pay, the wife is on the hook because her name was on the account, not the husband's.

Never have a joint bank account or credit card. If you made the mistake of opening a joint account, close it. If a divorce is imminent, you should immediately contact joint credit card companies, in writing, to freeze or cancel your joint accounts. You do not want to be responsible for your spouse's new credit card charges, particularly when those charges may include attorney's fees. This also protects your credit rating. It's important to remember that, although a creditor may freeze a joint account, the outstanding balance must be paid off before the account can be closed.

You should also close your joint bank accounts. If any proceeds are removed, keep a detailed accounting of where the money is placed or how the proceeds are spent. You will undoubtedly be asked for that accounting as part of the divorce process. You can save yourself time and money by keeping accurate records.

I had a client who made the common mistake of sharing a joint bank account with his wife during the marriage. My client was the chief breadwinner during the marriage, earning approximately $150,000 per year. The parties used this joint bank account as their operating account. In other words, my client would deposit his paychecks, as well as any other money he earned on his real estate investments, into this account. At the time he filed for divorce, there was more than $15,000 in that account.

When my client opened the first bank statement he received after he filed for divorce, he was horrified to see fifteen insufficient balance charges. We later discovered that on the day his wife was served with the Summons and Petition, she immediately went to the bank and withdrew the entire $15,000, not taking into consideration that there may have been outstanding checks written against the account. In the end, we were able to apply those charges to the wife's side of the property division, but my client had to pay me attorney's fees to fix the problem.

Establish your own credit. In a perfect world, I wouldn't encourage my clients to have their name on any credit card, or other monthly bill. In a divorce, the risks of being solely responsible for a bill tend to outweigh the benefits.

However, I also know how important it is to establish your own individual credit during the marriage so that if things go bad you will be able to land on your feet. One way to do this is to have your name listed on some of the household accounts, such as electricity, telephone, and cable. It is even okay to establish at least one credit card in your own name. This will help to create an individual credit history. When you are on your own, you will have a better chance qualifying for loans, mortgages, and credit cards. These are all important considerations after a divorce.

Although you'll certainly need to disclose it during the divorce process, there's no need to let your spouse know about this particular credit card account during the marriage. You can always have the statements sent to a P.O. box. Having at least one credit card in your name may help you to hire an attorney or relocate if necessary.

Discuss finances with your spouse. If your soon-to-be ex spouse is refusing to tell you all the details surrounding your financial lives, it will make it much easier for them to convince you they have disclosed all of your assets during the divorce process. If you don't know what questions to ask, it will make it easier for them to use all the legal methods at their disposal to hide their assets.

Make sure you are in charge of preparing the tax returns. Especially if you suspect your spouse of shifty behavior, insist on taking care of preparing your income tax returns. That will protect you from any trouble a vindictive spouse could start–on *your* behalf–with the IRS.

Have bank or investment account statements sent to you at work. If you think your spouse might be prone to bundling up your belongings–including important documents–and stuffing them down the garbage disposal or having a huge "my marriage is over" bonfire in the backyard, you'll want to consider storing the most critical paperwork at your office.

Never name your spouse as the beneficiary of your life insurance policy or any other investment accounts. As soon as the divorce process begins, both parties are automatically restrained by the provisions contained in the Summons, which generally states the following:

Neither party may dispose of any assets except for the necessities of life or for the necessary generation of income or preservation of assets, by an agreement in writing, or for retaining counsel to carry on or to contest this proceeding; neither party may harass the other party; and all currently avail-

able insurance coverage must be maintained and continued without change in coverage or beneficiary designation. If you violate any of these provisions, you will be subject to sanctions by the court.

That's an attorney's way of saying that once the divorce process begins, you can't change anything. This includes removing your spouse's name as beneficiary on your life insurance policy. Therefore, if a divorce is on the horizon, it's better to have already named somebody else as the beneficiary of your assets so you are not forced to violate the provisions contained in the Summons. If you don't, and you die during the divorce proceedings–which can stretch on for years in some cases–your soon-to-be ex-spouse will receive the insurance money. Is that really what you want?

Have a Power of Attorney. A power of attorney is a legal document, which is created for the purpose of allowing another individual to make legally binding decisions on your behalf, or vice versa. The two people creating this document are called the "principal" and the "agent." The principal designates the agent in the document, and the agent is authorized to act on the principal's behalf–to stand in the shoes of the principal for whatever business the power of attorney permits.

A power of attorney can be general, so the agent can conduct any sort of business on behalf of the principal, or it may be specific, limited to the transactions expressly provided for in the document. Third parties may treat the agent as if he or she is the principal in any transactions the agent is authorized to conduct. Powers of attorney are commonly used in all sorts of business activities and are very frequently executed on behalf of individuals.

I would suggest that you and your spouse execute these

agreements very early in your marriage. This will give you the ability to make unilateral decisions. However, it will give your spouse the same ability. Therefore, I suggest you keep both of the powers of attorney in a safe deposit box, to which only you have access, particularly if you suspect your spouse will abuse the advantages that the document provides.

I represented a wife in a divorce proceeding. She and her husband had been married twenty-three years. The husband earned approximately $180,000 per year, while my client had been a stay-at-home mother to their three children. As part of the judge's order, the parties were to sell their home and my client was to receive the entire net proceeds from the sale, approximately $50,000. When we arrived at the closing, the husband failed to appear. Instead, he sent the couple's eighteen-year-old son in his place.

Apparently, the husband had executed a power of attorney, which granted his son the right to appear and sign the documents in his place. Unfortunately, the husband had instructed his son not to sign the closing documents, unless he was given one-half of the net proceeds, which was in direct violation of the court's order.

After several hours of attempting to convince the eighteen-year-old son he was making a mistake, I had no choice but to contact the judge directly. The judge told everyone that if the parties' son refused to sign the closing documents, as drafted, she [the judge] was going to send a sheriff to the closing and have the boy arrested for violating a court order. Of course, my client started crying hysterically at the thought of her son being put in jail. Still, the husband continued to instruct his son not to sign the documents.

Eventually, my client relented and agreed to give the husband half of the proceeds and save her child from going to jail. All of this could have been avoided if my client had a power of attorney, which had been executed earlier by the husband, giving her the authority to conduct general business on his behalf.

Keep non-marital assets separate. Don't be fooled into thinking "what's mine is ours and what's hers or his is ours." It is this kind of thinking that will get you crushed in a dispute over property division. What you have to remember is that non-marital assets are not part of the property that is divided in a divorce. Instead, they are considered the exclusive asset of either the husband or the wife and generally awarded to that person in a divorce proceeding. Categories of non-marital assets include, but are not limited to, the following:

* property you inherit;

* proceeds from personal injury awards (such as worker's compensation or accident proceeds);

* items owned prior to marriage; and

* gifts to one party rather than both parties.

If non-marital assets are co-mingled with assets purchased or improved during the marriage, it may not be possible to claim the asset as yours in the event of divorce. However, some tracing of non-marital assets may be possible. For example, if a non-marital asset is sold during the marriage and the proceeds from the sale are used to purchase another asset, it may be possible to trace a non-marital interest in the new asset. For example, if a car owned before a marriage is sold during the marriage and the proceeds are used to purchase a new vehicle, you may be able to claim a non-marital interest in the new vehicle. To do so, it is very important to retain all documents demonstrating the sale of the asset and the use of the proceeds realized from the sale.

Tracing of non-marital assets is becoming a larger part of the divorce process, due in part to the fact that many people are getting married later in life—and therefore have the ability to create more wealth on their own before getting married. Another consideration is the trillions of dollars of assets that are being inherited by today's baby boomers.

These numbers can be very, very significant. I recently had a "two-wheeler cart case," where there were so many boxes of documents, we had to stack them on a two-wheeler cart to carry them around. After several months of work, we were able to determine that $1.8 million of a 2.5 million-dollar-estate was related to either non-marital or premarital assets.

It's tedious, it's time-consuming, and it's expensive, but for $25 thousand dollars or so, my client was able to say, "This $1.8 million is not part of the marital estate."

Become a Pack Rat. The easiest way to trace your non-marital assets is to provide documentary evidence that the money was kept separate from marital investments. In order to do so, you will need to save all receipts, bank statements, credit card statements, tax returns, and all other financial documents. Remember that a lot of financial institutions will destroy records after a certain number of years, making reproducing the document impossible.

I represented the wife of an extremely successful businessman. At the time of the marriage, the parties entered into a prenuptial agreement, which specifically listed all of the financial holdings of the husband. My client had nothing at the time of the marriage. The parties stayed married for fourteen years. At the time of dissolution, the husband tried to argue that the financial assets could be directly traced to the assets in existence at the time of the marriage. If he would have been successful in his claim, he would have succeeded in proving that all of his existing assets were non-marital. The result would have been that the husband walked away with $2.5 million worth of assets and my client would have emerged with less than $100,000.

Fortunately for my client, and unfortunately for the husband, he didn't keep the documents mentioned above and the financial institutions had destroyed all of their records. Although the husband testified as to what he believed happened to his initial investments, the court found his testimony to be insufficient and divided all of the financial assets evenly between the parties.

In a subsequent case, a husband claimed he received his interest in the family business from his father. But–too bad for him–he didn't keep any documentation. Remember, when you're claiming a non-marital interest, it is your burden of proof, and if you can't prove it, then you don't get the benefits. If you don't have the documentation, you don't get the credit. It cost the husband nearly $300,000 of assets.

Don't co-mingle. The "co-mingling" of funds is a huge roadblock to making a claim that money belongs to you and not your spouse. Keeping the money in separate, segregated accounts is so important. Do not co-mingle non-marital money into your joint checking account. In other words, do not keep it in an account where you also deposit your payroll checks. Those are critical things people just don't think about.

It's not as simple as being able to withdraw from your joint account the amount of, say, an inheritance you received, and then splitting the rest. If you inherited $100,000 from your great aunt and you put it into your joint account, you can't just take out $100,000 when you get a divorce. It's co-mingled, so it's possible that the inheritance can now be considered marital property. Or, if you use the money to buy stock, you might be stuck with only a percentage of the stock you bought, because there was other marital money in your account, too.

The law is extremely precise when it comes to co-mingled funds. You don't have to trace serial numbers on dollars, but close to it.

When it comes time to prove your non-marital claims, or trace an asset back to its non-marital origins, it will be very helpful if you have the original receipt. In fact, it is very helpful if you keep *all* of your receipts and records, which will allow you to support your non-marital claims at some time in the future. I suggest you set up a file cabinet, containing hundreds of hanging files, broken down by the individual asset purchased, and its corresponding tracing documents. Hang on to everything. By the way, it is probably best to keep such a file cabinet in a safe, undisclosed location until the time of the divorce. If you keep it in the garage at home, it may raise some suspicions.

Document gifts. Whenever you receive a gift that's intended for you alone, be sure to ask that person to fill out a "donor intent form." I suggest limiting this to gifts with a value of more than $1,000. This form will provide documentary evidence that the gift was intended for you alone, and not for you and your spouse jointly. This document can then be used at the time of dissolution to prove the non-marital character of those items.

Of course, have the gift giver fill out the form at the time they give you the present and not fifteen years later. Most judges will not give too much weight to a donor intent form that was filled out fifteen minutes before the parties walk into the courthouse. Be sure to keep the donor intent form in a safe place.

Here's an interesting exception to the gift rule. In most states, the engagement ring is considered a non-marital item of property, which will not be considered at the time of property division. In other words, when your attorney is preparing a list of marital property to be divided, the engagement ring won't be included and will simply be given to the wife.

I once worked for an attorney representing a husband who wasn't exactly thrilled his wife was going to get to keep her engagement ring. The "loving" husband that he was, he offered to have all of his wife's jewelry cleaned, including the engagement ring, some time prior to filing for divorce. On his way, he stopped at the jewelry store and had the 2.5-carat diamond replaced with a nearly worthless cubic zirconium. He matched it perfectly, and when it came time to divide the personal property, the husband made a huge deal about his ex-wife being able to keep the engagement ring, all the while chuckling under his breath at the elaborate bait-and-switch he had pulled. The husband never told us about the stunt either. Eventually, the switch was discovered by his wife and the husband was ordered to reimburse the wife for the full amount of the original diamond.

A simple way to avoid this scenario is to purchase a less expensive engagement ring for the ceremonial purpose of dropping to one knee and proposing. Then, after you are married, feel free to spend as much money as you like on a "post-marriage" engagement ring. By doing so, you are creating a marital asset subject to division at the time of divorce.

Protect your inheritance. If your parents are aging–and wealthy–and you're in the process of a divorce, you might want to consider asking them to take some steps to protect your inheritance. Without proper planning, if your parents pass away while you're in the process of ending your marriage, your soon-to-be ex-spouse would be entitled to a portion of the inheritance. But if your parents set up what's called a discretionary, irrevocable trust in your name, the money is off limits to creditors, including your former spouse. One word of warning: As soon as you dip into the trust, the money becomes fair game. So wait until your divorce is finalized to access the inheritance.

Review your financial holdings regularly. Maintain complete and separate records of your financial holdings such as bank accounts, IRAs, 401Ks, land purchases, and stocks. This includes assets in your spouse's name as well. You may wish to maintain copies of these records at your place of employment or in a safety deposit box in your name only. Records have a way of disappearing after a divorce has been started.

Videotapes make great exhibits in court. This may seem a bit overboard, but it's a good idea to videotape the contents of your home on a regular basis. One of my clients learned this the hard way. He and his wife had not been getting along very well. While she was out of town for business, he decided to file for divorce. He also decided, without my knowledge, that it would make him feel better if he flooded the toilets in the house and smash all of the mirrors.

Prior to trial, the opposing attorney disclosed to me that his client, knowing how vindictive her husband could be, had made a videotape of the house prior to her business trip and then another videotape when she returned.

When I viewed the two videotapes, I knew my client would never want the judge to see these tapes. My client was forced to agree to pay a considerable amount of money to repair the property he had damaged as well as the wife's attorney's fees. Ouch.

Buy two of everything. This may seem a bit excessive, but when the court divides the personal property, they cannot give both people the same item. If you buy two of everything during the course of your marriage you can save yourself a lot of time and expense when dividing the personal property items.

If you've taken my advice and implemented some of these ideas early in your marriage, getting a divorce down the road will be a whole lot easier to deal with, especially on your pocketbook.

VII

The Great Custody Dispute

If you have children, this will probably be the most important chapter of the book. And even if you don't, there are plenty of lessons here that will apply to other aspects of the divorce process.

One study showed that more than one out of three divorced fathers had no access or visitation rights with their children. Equally disconcerting is that only one out of ten mothers say they value their ex-husband's input when it comes to handling problems with their kids. In fact, in another study, mothers rated teachers, doctors, close friends, and relatives higher than their ex-husbands when it came to questions regarding how to handle problems with their children following a divorce. From my own observations, things haven't changed much since that study was conducted. Divorce can be a difficult situation for everyone involved.

At the outset, I feel it's necessary to emphasize the negative impact a divorce has on children. Every year, millions of kids find themselves in a situation over which they have no control. These children often blame themselves for the failure of their parents' marriage. That is tragic.

Parents often get distracted by the strong emotions brought up during a divorce, which can divert their attention from concentrating on what's best for their children. It's a huge challenge for parents going through a divorce to be able to maintain some perspective on what their kids need, and how the kids will react to what the changes are in the family. It's easy for parents to miss that because their own feelings are so overwhelming. Some parents aren't able to separate what they're feeling from what their kids are feeling, and that can be a real challenge.

The stakes are high. And the purpose of some of the advice given in this book is not only to help prepare for a custody dispute, but to win such a dispute.

Nonetheless, I do not condone the use of children to get back at your spouse. Some parents say terrible things about their ex-spouse in front of the kids. Some parents keep their children from celebrating family events at the other parent's house. Some parents don't let their sons or daughters participate in extracurricular activities, just because the other parent encourages them. This type of behavior can be severely detrimental to your kids. Don't do it.

There are several excellent books written specifically about how to help your children cope with the divorce process. If you're tempted to use your kids as bargaining chips or pawns to achieve your agenda, I strongly encourage you to read one of those books or talk to an expert before you cause permanent damage to your children. I have included a list of those books in Appendix B.

How the Court Determines Custody

Before you can prepare for your custody dispute, you need to become familiar with the rules of the game. In other words, it's important to understand the applicable laws used by the courts. I have included a table in Appendix C that summarizes the law in each of the fifty states as it relates to custody.

In every divorce case involving a child, the court, or the mother and father, if they are able to reach an agreement, must make a determination regarding "physical" and "legal" custody.

LEGAL CUSTODY

Legal custody deals with the right to be involved in major life decisions affecting the child. If the parties have joint legal custody, which is preferred in most states, they have equal rights and responsibilities over medical decisions, school decisions, and religious upbringing. Legal custody also allows the parent access to school and medical records.

PHYSICAL CUSTODY

On the other hand, generally speaking, the parent with *physical* custody has control over the routine daily care, and the primary residence, of the minor child. Joint physical custody means that the routine daily care and residence of the child is equally structured between both parents. Most states, however, have laws that specifically state that an award of joint physical custody is not preferred. Generally speaking, the courts shy away from joint physical custody because of the belief that a child should have one primary home and not be bounced back and forth between the parents.

LIST OF FACTORS

When making the decision regarding which parent should have physical custody, the court must determine what is in the best interest of the child. In order to do so, the court will analyze several factors. Each state has its own list of factors. However, generally speaking, these factors will include some combination of the following:

* The wishes of the child's parents about custody. This can be as simple as what each parent wants with respect to custody. In order to increase your chances of getting what you want, *you should always ask for sole physical custody*. Remember, you will never get more than what you ask for. You can always settle for joint physical custody later on in the case. In fact, it will look like you were making concessions by settling.

* The reasonable preference of the child, if the court deems the child to be of sufficient age to express preference. Most states do not have a minimum age at which the courts will consider the child's preference when making a determination of custody. Despite what you might hear, there is no requirement that the child must be a certain age in order to have an input. Instead, whether the court will consider a child's input will greatly depend on the maturity level of the child. This does not mean that the child will have the final say; it only means that the court will take the child's opinion into consideration when making a decision.

Be advised that when the child reaches a certain age, he or she will likely "vote with their feet." In other words, when a child becomes a teenager, it will no longer matter what the custody designation may be; they will probably choose to live with whichever parent they prefer. Keep in mind that the child is still bound by the original ruling until the non-custodial parent requests the custody situation be changed and the court agrees.

I have handled hundreds of cases in which a non-custodial parent makes a request to modify custody based upon their teenage child's desire to no longer live with the custodial parent. Under those circumstances, the court will pay much greater attention to the preference of the child.

* **The child's primary caretaker.** This is probably the most critical factor when determining which parent should be awarded physical custody of a child. The court will try to determine which parent did the grocery shopping, made the beds, put the children to bed at night, arranged play dates, and took the children to their doctor and dentist appointments. Therefore, it is important you involve yourself with these duties from the moment your child is born. Most courts will agree that all else being equal, the primary caretaker will be awarded custody of the child. I will discuss this factor in greater detail later in this book.

* **The intimacy of the relationship between each parent and the child.** Under this factor, the court will examine the relationship of each parent with the child. For example, which parent does the child confide in when they have problems at school or with a boyfriend or girlfriend? As a parent, and a soon-to-be-divorced mother or father, be sure to keep the lines of communication open with your child. You want to make sure your child is as comfortable talking to you about sex as they are talking about music.

* **The relationship of the child with a parent and other people who might significantly affect the child's best interests.** The court takes into consideration the relationship your child has with grandparents, siblings, or anyone else who may affect their lives. The better the relationship you

have with your extended family, the better it will look to the court when making a custody determination.

I recently handled a case where my client was seeking sole physical custody and the other side was asking for joint physical custody. After months of investigation and painstaking interviews, the court determined that my client's close relationship with her parents, siblings, and cousins was an important factor in the life of her child and awarded her sole physical custody.

If possible, try to live near your family. In addition, it may also be helpful if you have a history of spending vacations and holidays with your side of the family.

* The length of time the child has lived in a stable, satisfactory environment and the desirability of maintaining continuity. This factor specifically addresses the importance of stability for the child. The more stable your home environment, the more likely it will be that you will be awarded sole physical custody. It is exactly for that reason it is extremely important to remain living in the family homestead. As soon as you move out, you lose the upper hand on this particular factor. Obviously, the person continuing to reside in the family home has a better argument for stability and continuity. *Therefore, never leave the family home without your children, with the intention of changing residences.*

I had a client come to me several months after his wife initiated the divorce process. He had already moved out of the family home and was living in an extended-stay hotel. His wife remained in the family home with their three children, all under the age of seven. When I asked him why he had moved from the family home, he replied, "She served me with divorce papers. I no longer wanted to live under the same roof." When I explained to him that he was under no obligation to leave the family home and that, in fact, leaving might have jeopardized his ability to obtain custody of his children, he immediately returned to the family homestead.

Upon his return, his wife's attorney filed a motion with the court, asking that my client be removed from the family home. I argued that my client had as much right to remain in the family home as did his wife, and that it would be a waste of family finances for my client to be forced to stay at a hotel. The court agreed, and ordered that both parties could remain in the family home until the divorce proceeding was final. In the end, my client was awarded joint physical and joint legal custody of his children.

* **The mental and physical health of all individuals involved.** Under this factor, the court is authorized to require all parties undergo extensive psychological testing, including, but not limited to. the Minnesota Multiphasic Personality Inventory-2 (MMPI-2). The MMPI-2 is the most frequently used clinical test across the country. It is used quite often in court cases to provide personality information on defendants or litigants in which psychological adjustment factors are pertinent to resolution of the case. Make sure your attorney is familiar with the MMPI-2 test and is comfortable interpreting the results.

You should also become familiar with the *Diagnostic and Statistical Manual of Mental Disorders, Fourth Edition (DSM-IV)*. The purpose of *DSM-IV* is to provide "clear descriptions of diagnostic categories in order to enable clinicians to diagnose, communicate about, study, and treat people with various mental disorders." This is the "bible" of mental disorders; it includes details on everything from Attention Deficit Disorder to Schizophrenia.

You can use the information you gain from reading the *DSM-IV* to explain to the custody evaluator, or the judge, how strangely your soon-to-be ex-spouse has been behaving. You don't need to be an expert; you just need to know some of the symptoms and terminology in order to guide the experts in the right direction.

* The child's cultural or religious background. Generally, this factor comes into play only if the two parents have different cultural backgrounds (for example, an interfaith marriage). Therefore, in order to increase your chances of being awarded sole physical custody, take steps to ensure you are raising your child with your religious beliefs and not exclusively those of your spouse.

* The effect on the child of the actions of an abuser, if related to domestic abuse that has occurred between the parents. Obviously, if there has been domestic abuse, it is very unlikely that the abuser will be awarded sole physical custody. In fact, in some states, the courts are precluded from even awarding joint physical custody if there has been domestic abuse between the parties or abuse involving the children.

* The willingness of each parent to encourage and permit frequent and continuing contact by the other parent with the child. In the past few years, a new concept has arisen in the arena of family law, more specifically involving custody disputes. This concept has been identified as "Parental Alienation." The Parental Alienation Syndrome (PAS) is defined as "the systematic denigration of one parent by the other with the intent of alienating the child against the other parent." The purpose of the alienation is usually to gain or retain custody without the involvement of the other parent. The alienation usually extends to the other parent's family and friends as well.

If the court believes one parent is intentionally alienating the child from the other parent, it usually has the discretion to take custody away from the parent engaged in the alienating behavior. At the very least, parental alienation will be a factor for the court to consider when making a determination as to custody. Therefore, do not engage in conduct that will interfere with your soon-to-be ex-spouse's relationship with your children. While it may seem you are punishing your soon-to-be ex-spouse, in reality you are harming your children and sabotaging your chances for custody.

WHAT IF I HAVE TO SETTLE FOR JOINT CUSTODY?

If it appears that sole custody is not an option, you should be aware that the court will generally consider some variation of the following additional factors when determining whether an award of *joint* custody is appropriate: the ability of both parents to cooperate in the rearing of their children, whether or not they have developed methods of resolving disputes regarding major decisions concerning the life of their children, and whether it would be detrimental to the child if only one parent were to have sole authority over the child's upbringing.

Therefore, if you are in the unenviable position of having to settle for joint custody, you will want to establish a pattern of making joint decisions with your soon-to-be ex-spouse, while at the same time making sure you carefully document any time he or she denies you the opportunity to be involved with those decisions.

Two Words: Be involved. This seems almost too easy. However, as stated earlier, every state has a list of factors the court considers when deciding the issue of custody, and every list includes the "primary parent" factor. The most important piece of being the primary parent is *involvement* in school and extracurricular activities. The following is a list of ways to be involved:

* **Make sure every teacher knows your name, and vice versa.** You do not want to be caught unaware of your children's teachers' names. In a recent case where I was representing the mother, I decided to take the father's deposition. Throughout the entire case, the father was claiming how involved he was in the children's schooling and education. During the deposition I asked him to name his children's teachers. He was unable to do so. The father's inability to identify his children's teachers by name went a long way with the judge when deciding who should have custody.

* **Make sure your children's coaches are aware of your involvement.** Even better, volunteer to coach one of your child's sporting teams. Always remember everyone is a potential witness. The more people you can impress with your involvement, the better off you will be during the divorce process.

* **Do the drop-offs and pick-ups at school or daycare.** Daycare providers and teachers can be the most compelling witnesses during a custody trial. The courts put a lot of weight into their testimony. Therefore, the more often you can show these people you are the parent responsible for dropping off and picking up the kids, the more likely it is they will testify on your behalf.

In every case where the child attends daycare or preschool, the first thing I will ask my client to obtain is the attendance record or sign-in book at the daycare or preschool. Most schools are required by the state to keep records of who is dropping off and picking up the child every day. The schools use this information to ensure that a child is being picked up by the proper person. In a divorce case, however, this information can be used to bolster your position for being the primary parent.

* **Be the parent to bring your children to the doctor whenever possible.** This gives you the opportunity to build a record. Every time you bring your child to the doctor, the clinic or hospital documents who brought the child. Although it's not the only thing a judge looks at, this can become a very important factor for the court in determining which parent is the primary caregiver.

In one recent case, both parents were claiming to be a little boy's primary caregiver. We subpoenaed his medical records, and the "brought by" area on the admission forms listed the mother as the person who brought him in during the vast majority of the visits. The mother was clearly the boy's caretaker, and the court used that information in making its decision. It granted sole physical custody to the mother.

* **If possible (and legal), record your conversations with your spouse.** The idea of tape recording conversations without your spouse's consent may seem distasteful, but keep in mind that almost every custody dispute becomes a matter of "he said, she said." Most of the time, the decision regarding which parent should be awarded custody comes down to credibility.

Remember, however, that it is illegal in most states to tape record conversations in which *you* are not a party. In other words, you can't tape record conversations between your spouse and her lover without the permission of at least one of the parties to the conversation. On the other hand, in most states it is perfectly acceptable to tape record your *own* conversations, even without the other person's knowledge.

I have provided a breakdown of the one party/two party telephone tape recording law in each of the fifty states in Appendix D. This information may have changed since the writing of this book, so you should always check the actual state law where you live and obtain advice from an attorney before recording any statement over a telephone line. It would appear that, if a telephone conversation crosses state lines, federal law would have jurisdiction.

I have advised clients to purchase a tape-recording device that simply attaches to their telephone. Most of these devices are voice activated and are available at a local electronics store. When their soon-to-be ex-spouse calls them, the device clearly picks up and records both sides of the conversation. I have found these tapes to be extremely useful during cross-examination.

* Think twice about going to therapy, either individually, or jointly, with your spouse. I believe Samuel Goldwyn said it best. "Anyone who goes to a psychiatrist should have his head examined." In the context of a custody dispute, everything you say, or have said, to your therapist can, and will, be disclosed. Believe it or not, the client-patient privilege can be broken. All of those confessions you may have made over the years regarding your ability to parent, or your infidelities, become fair game for your spouse to use against you.

Don't make the mistake of making a therapeutic confession that will come back to haunt you many years later. While this advice may seem contrary to solving your marital problems, you must remember this book is not about saving your marriage; it is about controlling the divorce process.

I represented the husband in a recent case. They had been married for ten years, with a nine-year-old and a four-year-old. The wife served divorce papers because the husband had been having affairs. It was an ugly situation. During the process, we discovered something the wife told a doctor in an old medical record. The details weren't there, but we could see it had something to do with paternity.

Of course, my client wanted to know what that was about, so we dug a little deeper. Turns out that neither of the two kids were his—they were from two separate men, both of whom were married to other women. Unfortunately, this destroyed my client's relationship with his children.

Bottom line: Be careful what you tell your doctor. You may think you're protected by doctor-patient privilege, but all of that becomes relevant in a divorce process as discoverable, at least when kids are involved. If you don't have kids, it has no bearing whatsoever, because it has nothing to do with division of property. But if there are children involved and custody is an issue or access time is an issue, then everyone's mental and physical health becomes an issue. You can dig up medical records from ten or fifteen years ago about things someone said to therapists or doctors.

We had a case that went to trial and one of the big elements was the fact that the husband admitted to a therapist he had been physically abusive to his wife. Every time he was abusive he would come in and talk to the therapist about it. However, he had been denying he was abusive throughout the whole divorce process. We got the records, and he was sunk. It turned everything around for my client. People were doubting her story because she never called the police, there were never any visible scars or bruises, and she never told any of her friends. The other side was accusing her of being a liar. The husband was probably thinking it was never going to come out. But it did.

Monetary secrets can be an issue, too. There are times when financial issues you might think are buried will come up. Attorneys hand information over to a forensic accountant, and they can connect the dots or follow the paper trail to determine whether someone is double-dipping or hiding income someplace. The right expert can usually find hidden money.

* Use every opportunity to show your spouse's friends what a great parent you are. During a custody trial, each party will parade a litany of witnesses before the court. You can be certain that your soon-to-be ex-spouse will call her friends to testify about what a wonderful parent she is and what a lousy parent you are. With some careful planning, you can derail this testimony.

During the marriage, whenever you are socializing with your spouse's friends, be sure to volunteer to feed the baby and change the diapers. Another good way to show your spouse's friends what a great parent you are is to constantly mention the fabulous dinners you make for the family every night.

Be advised, however, that T.V. dinners and microwave popcorn do not necessarily qualify as a home-cooked meal. If you are not a great cook, I suggest starting out with some simple dishes. You certainly don't want to start out by burning the Thanksgiving turkey and giving your husband or wife something to laugh about with his or her friends, who may be potential witnesses during the divorce.

* If you travel, call the kids at school or daycare. Exhibiting good parenting skills in front of someone else makes sure there is a third-party witness. I once represented a client who traveled extensively for his job. The couple had two young children, ages four and two. Every morning, my client would call his children at daycare. He was aware of their schedules and made sure he called as soon as they arrived. The daycare providers were so impressed that they testified at trial on behalf of my client. Ultimately, the judge awarded my client joint physical custody of the children, with a fairly equal access schedule.

* Take every opportunity to be the primary caregiver. As I stated earlier in the book, this requires more than just allowing your spouse to sleep in. What good does it do unless other people know about it? Be sure to schedule early morning play dates for the kids or breakfast meetings with other friends with kids. This way, those people will see how involved you are in the parenting. Be sure to be on the lookout for opportunities to throw in seemingly off-handed remarks about how your absent spouse insisted on getting his or her beauty sleep or was just too tired to get out of bed.

* Encourage your spouse to take vacations with his or her friends, leaving the kids with you. This may seem like a lot of work, especially if you have more than one child. However, you will reap huge dividends during the divorce process. Be sure to keep meticulous notes regarding the length of these vacations and how many times your spouse called the kids–or didn't call–during those trips.

In fact, you can even offer to create a scrapbook for your soon-to-be ex-spouse upon his or her return. Be sure to include such things as solo plane tickets, single bedroom hotel stays, and any photographs of your husband or wife standing alone in front of whatever landmark they happened to be visiting on that trip. This seemingly kind gesture will have the dual benefit of appearing sentimental and documenting your spouse's selfish escape from childcare responsibilities.

* **Constantly update your affidavit.** An affidavit is a legal document that's submitted to the court during a dissolution proceeding. It is a sworn statement that contains facts about the marriage in order to support someone's request for relief. In most states, the parties are allowed to submit affidavits only in support of their requests for *temporary* relief. That means that until you get to a final trial, odds are that all of your statements will be submitted via affidavit.

A temporary hearing is used to establish ground rules to be followed throughout the divorce process. The court can make decisions regarding the temporary custody of the children, occupancy of the house, child support, and spousal maintenance. So, especially in the early stages of a proceeding, the affidavit becomes a critical document. Each spouse will use it to try and persuade the court that their position is stronger and should be accepted as truth.

Often, memories about an event will be a full 180 degrees off from each other. I, of course, only hear what my client believes happened, and the other attorney hears only what his or her client believes happened. Often, I think the truth lies someplace in between each person's memories. Memories are fallible, and emotions can cloud recollections. That's why it's critical to keep a written account of your life with your spouse.

When you give your affidavit to your attorney, he or she will take a look at it and pull out only the relevant entries, cutting away the things that aren't applicable. It's important not to make your affidavit too long. Shoot for a final length of between ten and fifteen pages. The judge is only going to read so much, and the key is to put the relevant stuff at the beginning.

Judges often have to remind attorneys to stay away from generalizations in affidavits. For example, don't say, "He was never home." Instead, document it like this: "On November 23, 2002, he didn't come home until 2:00 a.m. One of the kids was sick, so I had to bring her to the doctor by myself." Specific facts are very compelling to judges.

If you want to be able to submit an affidavit full of specific times, dates, and events, it's important to begin keeping a journal early in your marriage. Most people don't have the best memory, especially after years of marriage. Generally, by the time I sit down with my clients to prepare their affidavits, they have forgotten most of the critical information. The first thing I suggest, therefore, is they begin keeping a journal. Unfortunately, this journal will only help them keep track of current events.

I always wonder what it would be like if they had kept a journal since the time the guests started filing out of the reception hall. The journal would contain stories about how they argued on the way to the airport for their honeymoon about finances and whether or not they would wait to have children. It would contain all of the specific details, including arguments over who was getting up in the middle of the night to feed the baby, and who was responsible for changing those dirty diapers.

Most important, it would be filled with all of the stories about when Mommy forgot the baby in the car seat and sent her through the carwash, or when Daddy decided that it would only take a second to run into the dry cleaners to pick up his laundry, while Junior was sound asleep in the running car.

Make sure that you keep this journal in a very safe and private place, and be sure to update it regularly.

* **Never use your home computer when surfing the Internet.** You can't assume you have any privacy with respect to the use of your home computer. The number of divorces involving a spouse being caught using chat rooms or downloading pornography has increased dramatically over the past several years. No matter how many times you empty your computer's trash or delete your Internet history, someone will be able to reconstruct which sites you have visited or what has been downloaded.

We've had times when we've found things on computers that people thought were long gone. My client had a feeling her husband was dealing in child pornography, so before she filed for divorce she authorized a data recovery service to come in and take a look at their home computer. In this case, timing was everything. Had we filed for divorce before we went sniffing around, the husband probably would have destroyed the computer to protect himself. This way, he didn't suspect his wife was on to him. The data the experts recovered proved the husband was indeed involved with child pornography and won my client full custody of her children.

I represented a father in a custody dispute. My client wanted to have joint physical and joint legal custody, but the other side would not budge. The client suspected his wife was having an affair over the Internet, so as part of the discovery process, we sent in a computer technician to scan the family's home computer. What we found was astonishing. Our expert was able to retrieve hundreds of pages of pornographic material, which had been downloaded onto the family's computer and then erased.

In addition, because she was a stay-at-home mom, we were able to determine that my client's wife had been viewing extremely graphic material while she was supposed to be watching their two young children. My client was awarded sole physical custody, with a very liberal access schedule for mom.

* **Never apologize (in writing).** Whoever said "Love means never having to say you're sorry" was probably a divorce lawyer. If you have done something inappropriate, stupid, or insensitive, it is okay to say, "I'm sorry." Just don't put your apology in writing. You would be surprised at how many times a written apology makes its way into court as an exhibit.

In addition, you should also avoid any written praise of your spouse, especially when it comes to his or her parenting ability. I represented the wife in a case where both she and her husband worked outside the home. Both insisted that they were the primary caretaker and should be awarded sole physical custody of their children. Both paraded numerous friends, family members, and teachers before the court in order to prove they were indeed more worthy of the custody award.

Thankfully, my client had saved every birthday card, every Valentine's Day card, and every anniversary card she received from her husband during the eight-year marriage. We used these cards as exhibits at trial, which contained hand-written notes from the husband stating what a great mother my client was and how much he appreciated all of the hard work she did planning the children's meals, getting them to school, and arranging their social calendars. In the end, my client was awarded sole physical custody.

* Think twice about dating during a divorce. Most states today are what we call "no-fault" divorce states. What this means is that you no longer need to prove infidelity, abandonment, or abuse to get a divorce.

Today, however, most states have adopted the idea of "equitable distribution of property," which means that all of the marital property acquired during the marriage, regardless of whose name it is in, is divided evenly, or at least equitably, between the parties. (This doesn't include non-marital property that you–and not your spouse–might have received as a gift or inheritance.)

Unless a spouse has been inappropriately sexual with their new lover in front of the children, infidelity should have no effect on the final outcome of the divorce process. However, I have certainly found that there still exists an implicit bias, in the court system, against women who have extramarital affairs. Prior to 1970, a woman accused of adultery could lose her home, her income, and even her children. To some extent, that's still the case, even today. This may be because the judges are still predominantly men, or because there is still somewhat of a societal acceptance of men having affairs, but not women.

Another thing to consider is the impact it will have on your soon-to-be ex-spouse. In other words, imagine how difficult it will be to reach a settlement with your spouse if you are openly dating another person. In my experience, this type of behavior has not led to any decrease in animosity, and only serves to increase the length of time, as well as the cost, of the proceedings.

Bottom line, if you can wait until the divorce is finalized to introduce your new lover to all of your friends, relatives, and especially your children, it may serve you well to wait.

* **Congratulations, Daddy?** Almost every state has a law that deals with what's called "presumed parentage." In other words, if a child is born during a marriage, it is presumed that the husband is the biological father. This is very convenient—if it's actually true. However, if it is not true, then some unsuspecting husband could be on the hook financially until his non-biological child reaches the age of emancipation, which is generally eighteen years of age. Therefore, if you and your wife have dark hair and dark eyes, and your son has blonde hair and blue eyes, you might want to make a not-so-subtle request for a blood test.

I recently had a case that dealt with this exact issue. The couple had been married for sixteen years. During that time, they had a brief two-year separation, followed by a reconciliation. While separated, the wife had sex with another man and, as a result, had a child. My client, because the two were married, was legally presumed to be the father. In other words, my client had all of the legal and financial obligations for the child, even though he was not the biological father.

Two years after the child was born, the biological father committed suicide, without ever legally acknowledging the fact that he was the biological father. When my client came to me, the child was one week away from turning three years old. In most states, a presumed father must bring a petition to disprove his parentage no later than the child's third birthday. We quickly scrambled to prepare the paperwork and file it with the court. As you can imagine, my client's wife was not very happy, but my client was not sure if his reconciliation was going to last forever. Three weeks later, I was hired by the same client to handle his divorce.

CHILD SUPPORT

Another critical factor when children are involved is child support. In some states, including Minnesota, support is calculated based solely upon the net income of the non-custodial parent. In other states, such as North Carolina, child support is calculated using a shared income approach, which takes into consideration the income and expenses of both parents.

Although the court considers many factors in determining the appropriate amount of child support, in the majority of cases, it's dictated by a state's Child Support Guidelines. In Minnesota and in several other states, there's a statutory cap set for payments. A non-custodial parent can also be required to contribute to childcare costs and a portion of the children's medical and dental expenses.

Understanding the laws in your particular state is the first step to being prepared for a divorce. I have included a table in Appendix E that summarizes the law in each of the fifty states as it relates to child support.

VIII

Abuse, Abduction, and Accusations

Even the best laid divorce plans can go askew. In some cases, children are abducted by a disgruntled and frustrated parent. In others, the amount of abuse already present in a marriage escalates. Or an angry spouse might make false claims about their husband or wife. My goal is to help you understand why these things happen and where to turn for help.

Abuse

According to the Department of Justice, two-thirds of all marriages will experience domestic violence at least once. Domestic violence is never acceptable under any circumstances, and when it occurs, its emotional effects, especially on children, can be extremely damaging. Some children will assume responsibility for the abuse, while others will develop low self-esteem and have difficulty interacting with peers and adults.

While abuse can have a disastrous effect on children, the environment that fosters the abuse can be even more damaging. Sometimes people focus on the events themselves without looking at the bigger picture. Domestic violence is a crime in all fifty states. Domestic abuse laws are in place at the federal, state, and local levels.

Using the Order for Protection (OFP)

The first step toward putting a stop to the abuse is filing for an Order for Protection. Generally, this requires a written statement from the person making the request, along with a formal request. Usually, these documents are prepared by the attorneys or a court-provided advocate. If the court believes there is enough evidence to grant the Order for Protection, you will proceed to an evidentiary hearing.

At that hearing, the alleged abuser will often be given three options: 1) stipulate that the abuse took place; 2) deny the abuse and proceed with the hearing; or 3) deny the abuse, but allow the Order for Protection to be issued anyway. *If you're accused of abuse by your spouse, you should always proceed with the evidentiary hearing.*

If you allow the Order for Protection to be issued, you are greatly jeopardizing your ability to obtain custody of your children. In fact, most states have laws that specifically prohibit the court from awarding joint custody if there has been any incidence of domestic abuse between the parties. In addition, if an Order for Protection has been issued against you, even if it's completely without merit, it may affect your ability to possess a firearm or get a hunting license.

A very important thing to keep in mind is that in a proceeding for an Order for Protection, the court has the authority to exclude the abusing party from the dwelling the parties share (including the family homestead), award temporary custody, and establish child support payment.

All too often, these proceedings are used to get a leg up on the custody dispute. In other words, filing for an Order for Protection can be seen as a fast track to an award of custody. If an Order for Protection is filed against you, my advice is to fight it to the fullest extent of the law.

I was involved in a horrible case that took accusations of abuse to new levels of low—and nearly cost a child her life. The couple had just gone through a divorce and had agreed upon joint legal and joint physical custody of their two children, both teenage girls.

Everything went smoothly during the divorce process, but when the father got remarried, it all fell apart. The mother, as often happens when one spouse gets remarried and the other doesn't, started saying unsavory things about the new wife to the children. Her verbal barbs grew sharper and more aggressive, until the older daughter began to fall apart. She was torn between the fact that her dad loved his new wife, but her mom was saying terrible things about his new spouse. Her mother was also pressuring her to spy on the father and his new wife. The pressure continued to build, and the girl developed an eating disorder—and attempted suicide.

Then things got even worse. The mother accused the father of sexually molesting the oldest daughter, a classic case of Parental Alienation. The mother was trying to alienate the daughter against her ex-husband and his new spouse, and the daughter paid the price.

The girl didn't deny the charges; she was craving her mother's approval and played along. The girl even told her therapist that her father had tried to molest her, and, at the request of mother, the court issued an Order for Protection that barred the father from contacting his daughter. By the time I got involved, the daughter had tried to commit suicide five times and had not seen her father in six months.

Then she recanted her story. She told another therapist that her mother had made her say those things, and that she missed her father. It was almost a year before we were able to start establishing contact with the father. We had to start slowly. The happy ending is that the girl and her father have begun to heal their relationship, but they lost nearly two years of time together because of the false charges.

The moral of the story: Never, ever make kids feel as if they're choosing sides or that a divorce is their fault. Know that if you say bad things about the other parent, you're in effect saying bad things about your children. Even young kids–as little as two, three, or four years old–understand there are problems in a relationship, and it can affect them. They internalize it and can regress into bedwetting, problems with school, fighting, problems with grades, or worse.

If there is going to be an Order for Protection filed, make sure you are the one doing the filing. If you are unable to win the proverbial race to the courthouse, be sure to file a counter petition for your own Order for Protection.

Avoiding an Abduction

Parental abductions make up the majority of missing children in the United States. In 2001, there were about 725,000 children reported missing, or nearly 2,000 per day (although some of these did include runaways). The vast majority of these children were recovered quickly; however, the parent or guardian was concerned enough to contact law enforcement, and they placed the child into the FBI's National Crime

Information Center, a computerized national database of criminal justice information. It is available to federal, state, and local law enforcement and other criminal justice agencies. The Department of Justice reports that most of these abducted children were taken across state lines and concealed or their abductors prevented contact with the other parent or intended to keep the children indefinitely or to have custody changed.

Abducted children suffer emotionally and sometimes physically at the hands of abductor-parents. Many children are told the other parent is dead or no longer loves them. Uprooted from family and friends, abducted children often are given new names by their abductor-parents and instructed not to reveal their real names or where they lived before. Because of the harmful effects on children, parental kidnapping has been characterized as a form of child abuse.

If your soon-to-be ex-spouse refuses to return your child, you may seek relief under the Parental Kidnapping Prevention Act (PKPA), a federal law addressing parental kidnapping rights. Contact the local law enforcement authorities and request they assist in the return of the child. If they refuse, insist they enforce the PKPA statute. Local law enforcement is bound by law to enforce the PKPA, and it is not up to them to selectively enforce it or to decide the merits of any specific case or situation where the PKPA is applicable.

All fifty states and the District of Columbia—as well as Congress on a national level—have enacted civil and criminal laws to address parental kidnapping and interstate and international child custody and visitation disputes. Make sure you discuss with your attorney the remedies available in your jurisdiction.

Six risk profiles for abduction were identified in a research study by the Judith Wallerstein Center for the Family in Transition. The profiles are parents who:

- have threatened to abduct or abducted previously;
- are suspicious and distrustful due to a belief abuse has occurred and the parents have social support;
- are paranoid-delusional;
- are sociopathic;
- have strong ties to another country; or
- feel disenfranchised from the legal system (for instance, if they're poor, a minority, or victims of abuse).

Furthermore, mothers and fathers were equally likely to abduct their children, although generally at different times. Fathers were more likely to abduct when there was no child custody order, whereas mothers were more likely to abduct after the court had issued a child custody order.

I worked on a case where I represented the husband wo had been awarded temporary custody of his children. After dropping the children off at his wife's home, he returned later to find the house empty. Suspecting foul play, we called the airport and bus terminals. The airport security had stopped his wife at the airport trying to board a plane to Florida with the children. The mother had told the children to throw away all bags with their names on them because they were changing their names when they arrived in Florida. In addition, the wife had told the ticket agent that she had lost her identification and her name was Mary Poppins. Thankfully, this tipped off security and the children were returned safely to my client.

SAFEGUARDS

When there are factors present that indicate a heightened risk of child abduction, you should insist your lawyer request safeguards from the court that are appropriate to the facts and circumstances of the case. These may include, but are not limited to:

- **Restrictions on the removal of a child from the state or country.** Including a provision in the custody order limiting the right of the noncustodial parent to remove the child from the state and the country may help deter an abduction, but it is certainly not a foolproof solution.

- **Supervised visitation.** One of the most obvious ways to deter an abduction is to ensure your exspouse is supervised when he or she is with your child. The most common example of supervised visitation is allowing a parent to visit their child in what's called a "parent center," generally a clinical room in an office building where a social worker actually sits in the room with them while they talk or play. There are also other, less sterile visitation centers that are set up more like a comfortable home, which I'd recommend you investigate if you need to participate in supervised visitation.

Either way, it works like this: One parent drops off the child at the center then leaves, the other parent spends an hour or so with their son or daughter, and then the first parent returns to pick up the child. The center is a neutral location, so the two parents never need to see each other.

Supervised visitation can often be combined with other methods designed to determine whether a parent should receive access to his or her children. For instance, a "SCRAM™ bracelet" is a tool used in criminal cases, but a judge can also recommend its use in civil cases. It's an ankle bracelet that monitors your body's blood alcohol content, and it's connected via radio signal to your phone line. If you have a drink or try to tamper with the device, it sends a signal to a central agency that monitors the bracelet, who then contacts the other parent.

A judge suggested we use the SCRAM™ bracelet in a case I was working on. My client's wife was asking for access to their son, but she had a long history of drunk driving, including two DWIs with the child in the car. We all wanted to avoid having the mother and son meet in the sterile, often depressing environment of the parent center, but my client wasn't going to let his wife simply take the child–possibly in her car–without some precautions in place.

So she agreed to wear the bracelet to monitor whether she consumes any alcohol. If it ever goes off, she'll automatically forfeit her rights to have access to her son. So far, she's stayed clean, and my client's son has been able to have some good–and, more importantly, safe–time with his mother.

- **Specific visitation schedules.** The more specific the visitation schedule, the more difficult it will be for your soon-to-be ex-spouse to disobey the order. Try to avoid terms such as "reasonable and liberal" or "as agreed upon by the parties." Another problem of nonspecific schedules is that if a schedule is vague or ambiguous, the police will not be able to enforce the order.

- **Passport restrictions.** If you're concerned that your ex-spouse will take your child out of the country, you should contact the Department of State, Office of Passport Services at (202) 955-0337 (1111 19th Street N.W., Suite 260, Washington, DC 20522-1705) and request notification if a passport application for the child is made, and further request that a passport for the child not be issued. It is most efficient to fax the request, along with a copy of the custody order, to the passport services office. The fax number is (202) 955-0230.

- **Bonds to be posted for traveling out of the state.** The noncustodial parent may be directed by the court to obtain a bond in a large enough sum to act as a financial deterrent to child abduction. If an abduction occurs, the proceeds of the bond generally go to the aggrieved parent. The funds are useful in searching for the abducted children and in hiring legal counsel to enforce custody orders. Custodial parents who obstruct visitation rights may also be required to post bonds. Bonds may not be available in all states.

Keep in mind that very few judges have extensive experience with parental kidnapping cases. As a result, judges generally are wary about ordering protective measures absent a strong showing of the likelihood of flight. Be prepared to make your case strongly, or you will not receive the relief you are requesting.

While these safeguards are designed to make it far more difficult for a disgruntled ex-spouse to flee with a child, the reality is that parental abductions still occur. Here are some additional steps you can take ahead of time which can make it easier to locate a missing child as quickly and safely as possible.

- Communicate with your children about their fears and concerns regarding your ex-spouse.
- Make sure your children know their names, address, and telephone number.

- Teach your children how to use the telephone and how to make a long-distance call, or how to dial 911 to reach the authorities.

- Contact your local or state police departments to find out if they offer a child safety program that includes fingerprinting.

I suggest using a program such as IDENT-A-KID™ for each of your children. This service, and others like it, will provide you with a laminated, photo identification card complete with your child's name, fingerprint, date of birth, height, weight, and color of hair and eyes—plus your name and address. I recommend you have several cards made for each of your children; keep one with you at all times and give one to a relative or close friend or anyone that watches your child on a regular basis. You can learn more about this service at www.ident-a-kid.com.

Another very effective program is SmileSafe Kids, developed by school photography studio Lifetouch and the National Center for Missing and Exploited Children (NCMEC). The program partners with more than 30,000 schools across the country to offer free Safety IDs for families to use in emergencies. But more importantly, it works as a rapid response system that allows Lifetouch to provide a child's image to NCMEC in the event of an abduction, twenty-four hours a day, seven days a week, as long as the request is made and verified by the child's parent or guardian.

According to NCMEC, one in six children featured in their photo distribution program has been recovered as a direct result of someone recognizing the child's photo and notifying authorities.

I have included further information on parental abduction support agencies in Appendix F at the end of the book.

IX

Working with Experts

A divorce trial is often a parade of one expert after another, each testifying to a different aspect of your life and the lives of your children. It's best to learn how to work with these experts *before* the divorce process even begins. By doing so, you will be better prepared when the time comes for them to work on your case.

Accountants are used to prepare cash flow analysis, review tax returns, prepare spousal maintenance and child support calculations, and prepare a non-marital tracing. Appraisers are often used to determine the value of a business, the fair market value of a parcel of real estate (usually the homestead), or the resale value of personal property. The list goes on and on.

Here's a quick look at some of the most commonly used experts and what they can bring to the proceedings:

1. Custody/Access Evaluator

For most people with children, the most important expert is the custody/access evaluator. This is the person with the responsibility of making a recommendation to the court as to which party should be awarded custody and access of the children. You should expect to pay an initial retainer of anywhere from $3,000 to $5,000 for these experts, depending on their credentials. These evaluators will charge an hourly rate of up to $300 per hour, again depending on their experience and expertise. I believe it is important to use someone with extensive experience with children in divorce, preferably a child psychologist. Do not be fooled by the high hourly rates charged by some of these professionals. Just because they charge a higher rate does not make them a better qualified evaluator.

Some of the larger counties will provide a court-appointed evaluator at very little cost to the parties. However, generally speaking, like many public employees, these evaluators are overworked, underpaid, and some may even be unqualified. You are better off hiring a private evaluator; this is not the place to try to save a few bucks. Do not, however, think that hiring a private evaluator affords you the opportunity to unduly influence their decision. Personal contact with the evaluators, unless solicited by the evaluator, is strictly forbidden. In fact, any such attempts may undermine the evaluator's ability to do his or her job.

Try to avoid the hired gun type of evaluator. You want to make sure you hire someone with impeccable credentials and a reputation for being fair and impartial. You can be certain the judges are familiar with which evaluators are credible and which ones will render an opinion in favor of whomever is paying their bill. **Your attorney should have a list of which evaluators to use and which ones to avoid.**

In a custody/access evaluation, an evaluator meets with the parties and evaluates the custody/access issues based on the factors for determining custody that are spelled out in the statutes. Once the custody/access evaluation is complete, the evaluator submits a report to the court, which will recommend a custody and access schedule the evaluator believes is in the children's best interests.

Again, "best interests of the children" are magic words in custody proceedings. It's the standard that is used to make custody decisions. What is in the best interests of the children is determined by looking at several factors specified by the laws of each state. (You will find a list of those factors discussed earlier in this book, in Chapter VII, "The Great Custody Dispute.") This report is a critical element of your case.

The evaluator's report an assessment of each parent and their strengths as a parent, how they fit with the personality and needs of their child—what they bring to the parenting table, so to speak. The report becomes part of either the settlement negotiations or part of what the judge would receive if it all goes to trial. Typically, attorneys will use the results of that report to go through another round of negotiations.

Although custody studies may be challenged in court, many judges defer to the recommendations of the evaluator because, unlike the mother and the father, they are deemed to be an independent witness without any personal interest in the outcome. As a result, how you relate your case to the evaluator is very important. Therefore, early preparation for the evaluation is a key to a favorable recommendation.

The custody evaluator often has broad power to require psychological testing, chemical dependency evaluations, and urinalysis tests. How you interact with the custody evaluator may be a critical element of your custody case.

Here are some tips to keep in mind when working with a custody evaluator:

- Custody evaluators will often make you believe they agree with your side of the case. This is done so you drop your guard. **Never assume the evaluator's report will favor your position.**

- Custody evaluators are also people. That means they react to personalities. You are best able to present your case to an evaluator if you **appear open and honest.**

- **Do not argue** with the evaluator. Don't swear at them, either. Make eye contact and listen when they speak. This establishes a connection. It may help to nod your head as they speak, even if you disagree with what they are saying. When you disagree, tell them, "I see your point, but..." or "I agree, but would you consider this to be important...?"

- The custody evaluator doesn't care about "good guys" or "bad guys." The evaluator cares about what is in the **best interests of the children.** To relate your case to the evaluator, you must speak his or her language. Your statements must relate in some way to what is best for the children, not the parent. For example, the statement, "My husband is never home," is incomplete. It doesn't relate how his absence affects the kids. Always relate how the conduct affects the kids. A better statement would be, "My husband is never home. Because of that, the children have a better bond with me. He spends little time with the children and is unable to help them with their homework."

- Provide the evaluator with the **documents** supporting your statements (if applicable). These documents may include plane tickets, hotel receipts, medical records, and e-mails.

- Provide the evaluator with the **names of collateral contacts,** people who are aware of your strong points as a parent and your spouse's weak points. (It is usually better not to include too many relatives as part of your contacts since they may be perceived as having a bias.) The best collateral contacts are usually unrelated professionals, such as teachers, doctors, or therapists.

- **Always assume** when you go to court or visit a custody evaluator that you may be ordered to provide a urine sample for testing to determine if you have used drugs or alcohol.

CUSTODY STUDY ELEMENTS

Although each custody/access evaluator may have a slightly different approach to performing custody evaluations, there are some things you should expect:

* **Initial interview with evaluator.** At the initial interview, the evaluator will discuss at length the past history of care of the children. The evaluator will attempt to determine who was the **primary caretaker. Be prepared.** At the initial interview, arrive prepared with a chronology of events clearly set out. Don't assume you will be able to recall all of the facts during your interview. It is better to be overprepared.

* **Home visits.** The evaluator will make at least one home visit to watch you interact with your children. The evaluator is watching to see:

- Whether you actively play with and interact with your children;

- Whether you set appropriate boundaries for the children and whether they obey those boundaries;
- Discipline used;
- The children's reaction to the parent; and
- Condition of the home environment.

* **Alcohol assessments.** Where there are allegations of alcohol or drug abuse, the evaluator may refer you to a counselor for a chemical dependency evaluation. It is important you cooperate in that process.

* **Psychological evaluations.** If there are allegations of mental, emotional, or anger problems, the evaluator may refer you to a counselor or psychologist for a psychological evaluation. Make sure you communicate with the evaluator or counselor regarding any and all appointments. Budget enough time to complete the testing that is required. Any efforts to impede the testing will appear in the evaluation, so it's important you cooperate.

WHAT YOU SHOULD TRY TO DEMONSTRATE

Always remember those five magic words in custody evaluations: **"best interests of the children."** Custody evaluators listen for issues that relate to that phrase. You should relate how each element of your proposal is beneficial to your kids. Wherever possible use phrases that mean "best interests of the children" without using those exact words. Using the exact words sounds too legalistic and prepared. Your statements should sound more natural.

There are certain things evaluators look for in their custody evaluation. You should discuss these issues with the evaluator truthfully since the evaluator will, to a degree, assess your credibility. The issues you should be prepared to raise are the following:

Primary Caretaker. Where have the children lived since birth? What was the extent of contact each parent had at each phase of the children's lives? What responsibilities did each parent have? The best way to support the contention that you provided care for the children is through independent documentation. The other parent will no doubt contradict your assertions that you provided much of the care. Some of these may sound familiar, based on tips outlined earlier in this book, but they bear repeating. Independent documentation may include:

Daycare or school records demonstrating drop off and pickups or attendance at parent-teacher conferences. Even if you don't have documents demonstrating attendance at school functions, at least verify the dates of the conferences and **familiarize yourself with the daycare providers' or teachers' names.** The more information you are able to provide in that regard, the more credible you will appear as an active parent.

I recently handled a custody case where I represented the mother. During cross-examination, the father could not remember the names of the child's daycare providers, the address of the daycare facility, or the telephone number. The court was not impressed and awarded my client sole physical custody.

Medical records may document which parent brought the children in for a medical or dental appointment. If you can acquire these records prior to meeting with the evaluator, do so.

Homework assignments or report cards may require a parental signature before they are submitted at school. That signature may provide independent verification that the parent reviewed or was actively involved in the children's schooling. Wherever possible, acquire and retain these documents. Provide them to the custody evaluator to support your claims that you were actively involved in the kids' schooling.

Be able to **talk about who the children's friends are** and what activities they enjoy in detail.

Stability. The evaluator will be interested in which parent is able to provide the greater stability for the children. Stability includes a stable residence and a stable job. You may wish to document the ways in which you have provided greater stability in the past. You obviously will not emphasize those areas that do not favor you.

To effectively present the areas where you have provided or are able to provide more stability, you may wish to create a detailed chart. Visual aids help to present a clear picture to the evaluator. For example, you might want to create a chronological chart regarding each parent's residence and how many times the children have changed residences or schools. You may also wish to create a summary of each parent's employment to demonstrate stable financial circumstances. **Independent verification is also very helpful**. Where possible, you may want to procure documents demonstrating residence changes such as leases, purchase agreements, or real estate taxes.

A few years ago, I represented a father in a custody dispute. My client lived in the suburbs of Minneapolis, while the opposing party lived in the country in a trailer home located only fifty feet from a very busy freeway. In order to illustrate the difference between the two proposed custodial homes, I obtained aerial photographs of the two locations and had them enlarged to 4 x 6 feet. This was a very powerful exhibit.

The aerial photograph of my client's home showed the *Leave it to Beaver*-type neighborhood, complete with a park, pond, and a local elementary school. On the other hand, the aerial photograph of the father's home showed only how remote his geographic location was. There was no other home within three miles and the nearest structure was an industrial-size propane tank for the gas station, which was also located on the father's property. My client was awarded sole physical custody.

Endangerment or neglect. If you are raising issues of endangerment, you must relate specific incidents. Endangerment may be physical, emotional, or developmental. A calendar may be helpful to document the dates of the incidents. Documentation can carry critical weight with this type of allegation.

Documents may include:

- Medical reports documenting injuries from abuse or lack of supervision;
- Medical reports documenting complications because of neglect, such as asthma from cigarette smoke or lice from lack of hygiene;
- Police reports relating to police calls to the other parent's home;
- Any child protection reports;
- Counseling records for the children or the parent;
- The other parent's criminal or driving record;
- The criminal or driving record of people who have significant contact with the children;
- School records that may document attendance problems, school performance problems, counseling issues, or erratic child behavior while in the other parent's care or after returning from the other parent's care.

REMEMBER: Endangerment only exists if you tie the other parent's conduct into the children's care and best interests. For example, if you allege the other parent has an alcohol problem, it only will be effective if you can relate specific incidents where the alcohol use or abuse affected the kids. For instance, "My husband passed out on the couch while the children played unsupervised." or "My wife drove the children in the car while intoxicated." These statements are far more effective than simply "my husband drinks."

PARENTING PLAN

The custody evaluator will want to know what your proposal is for parenting. You should be prepared with research, facts, and answers. You may wish to write out your answers to the following questions so your response seems thought out. Don't over-prepare; your response should not sound mechanical. The answers should include:

- Where will the children live? Why is that in the children's best interests?
- What school will the children attend? Why is that in their best interests?
- Where will the children go to daycare? Why is that in the children's best interests?
- What will your work schedule be? Will that allow you sufficient time to supervise the children?
- What type of access schedule do you propose for the other parent?
- How does that schedule provide stability?
- Why is that schedule in the children's best interests?

REMEMBER: The custody evaluator is also looking at which parent is more likely to facilitate contact with the other parent. If you appear to be an unreasonable obstructionist with regard to the other parent's contact, it may be used against you.

It is also important, in a custody proceeding, to maintain a notebook including dates that events occur relating to the care of your children. What is the daily routine? Who takes them to the doctor? Who takes them to school activities? List any concerns regarding the other party's parenting, including the method of discipline, drug use, alcohol use, disabilities, or neglect.

All of these elements are designed to give your custody/access evaluator as much information as possible to determine what's best for your kids. This information can also be used to further develop your Affidavit, which was discussed earlier in Chapter VII, "The Great Custody Dispute."

2. Parenting Consultant

This is a relatively new concept in the area of family law. The idea is to have a highly qualified individual, usually a psychologist, in place to answer questions from the parents or help them in making decisions. This person acts as a resource for the entire family. They will help the parents look at what is in their children's best interests. They may help the parents understand appropriate developmental behaviors, places to take the children based upon age and emotional needs, and how to help the children better react to the transitions between two households.

Lots of times parents appreciate being able to hear some developmental information about their kids. The parenting consultant will tell them, "Here's what three-year-olds are really understanding about this. You don't need to explain all the this-and-that's about this. If they hear the message, that will be enough for them." Parenting consultants help translate the realities of the situation into age-appropriate levels of information.

The parenting consultant must make a large commitment to the family, which involves direct work with the parents, contact with the children, and preparing reports for the attorneys, if necessary. You can expect to pay $125 to $200 per hour for these services. Generally speaking, these costs are split between the parties.

3. Parenting Time Expediter

Simply put, the role of a parenting time expediter is to help the parents interpret and carry out the terms of their access schedule. This person will not provide counseling, therapy, or vocational help to the parties. Most people will hire a parenting time expediter when they have a high degree of conflict in their post-divorce parenting relationship and are unable to make joint decisions regarding the children.

The advantage of using a parenting time expediter is that both parents are given a chance to express their concerns and desires regarding a particular issue. After receiving input from both parties, via e-mail, telephone conversations, group meetings, or any other means necessary, the parenting time expediter is given the authority to make binding decisions. This is a way for the parties to avoid the time and expense of bringing the issues back to the courtroom.

The parenting time expediters will not usually require a retainer fee, but they do charge a fee for each service that is provided; anywhere from $175 to $275 per hour should be expected. In other words, if you contact the parenting time expeditor in any manner, there will be a corresponding charge, based upon the amount of time it took to resolve the issue.

In order to achieve the best results when working with a parenting time expediter, you must realize they can be a great ally in this process. You must treat them with respect, and they'll likely treat you—and your wishes—with respect, too.

4. Accountant

Accountants can play a large role in painting an accurate picture of a couple's financial situation. They provide any number of vital services along the way, from determining cash flow and tracing non-marital assets, to determining income and calculating child support or spousal maintenance, to maneuvering through the elaborate field of divorce taxation.

I believe it is critical to have a trained accountant on your team, particularly when a couple's financial picture necessitates deep digging to get to the bottom of an issue.

What I tell people is that the overall divorce, in my opinion, is about getting to that next chapter of your life and feeling like the system didn't screw you over and that you didn't get taken to the cleaners. If I can use an accountant to shed light on the financial piece of that so people understand and feel comfortable with the financial outcome, then I've done my part.

5. Financial Planner

A financial planner can help someone going through a divorce get a handle on not only where he or she is financially, but help them chart a course to get where they want to be in the future.

A financial planner can work together with the client in putting together a full customized plan, which means looking at education funding if there are younger kids, budgeting, tax planning issues, retirement planning, estate planning issues, or whatever other things might be most important to them.

When you can help somebody who's going through a tough time in their life such as divorce come up with a few golden nuggets–if they can walk away from the divorce more educated about their finances and feeling like they have more control over where they are–it's a wonderful feeling. Utilizing the expertise of a financial planner is a great way to help achieve this goal.

6. Business Valuator

Interest in a business is typically one of the largest assets in a couple's portfolio, so it can end up being a very contentious issue. That's where a business valuator comes in.

According to the business valuators I have spoken with, there is no easy way to figure out exactly what a business is worth. It's very subjective, and usually requires a professional to figure that out. What are the assets of the business? What is the income of the business? How sustainable is the income? How dependent is the business on a particular person, maybe the owner, or a particular customer that might represent most of the company's business? Those are all risk factors an expert will look at when trying to calculate a value.

Your attorney should have a list of all of these experts in your area and will help you get in touch with them. Remember, they bring a considerable amount of expertise to the table, and can help you uncover information, find solutions, and better understand the process.

X

Appropriate Behavior Once the Divorce has Started

As emotionally draining as it can be, divorce doesn't have to be an entirely negative process, especially if you have followed some of the advice in this book. Going into a divorce with eyes wide open, keeping your impulses in check, and not forgetting to act like an adult go a long way toward making the process less taxing.

Here are some tips:

Be reasonable.

If you have followed the advice in this book while you were happily married, then there should be no reason to fight during the divorce process. The only people who win if you and your spouse are fighting during the divorce are the attorneys.

And don't hang everything up on the principle of a specific point of contention. A client's ex-husband was on the stand, broken down in tears, and my client just wouldn't budge. "I just want to see my kids one more day a month," he cried, and my client sat there with a smug, satisfied look on her face. Outside of court, I urged her to settle by compromising with her husband about visitation. "It's the principle of it," she said, determined not to let him win.

We spoke at length about just how much that principle was costing her, not only in the thousands of dollars of attorney's fees, but in the psychological damage the ongoing battle was doing to her, her soon-to-be ex-spouse, and her kids. She eventually relented. The result was a much better outcome for everyone, especially the kids.

Another case will go down in history as one of the silliest wastes of time I've ever been a part of. I call it the Yellow Screwdriver Case. It started as a fairly run-of-the-mill divorce case. I represented the husband, and he and his wife settled everything pretty quickly, including the often tricky issues of custody and child support.

But then the wife claimed the husband was keeping a yellow screwdriver that had been given to her by her grandfather. The husband claimed he never saw the screwdriver, and offered to pay her a sum of money to make up for it. She didn't bite. In fact, letters flew back and forth between sides for weeks, and we couldn't settle on the personal property issue until this was dealt with. The wife kept accusing the husband of having the screwdriver, and the husband kept denying it. So, believe it or not, we went to trial.

I remember the judge looked at us like we were dressed in clown suits. We sat there for two hours testifying about tools. The wife continued to accuse the husband of knowing where the screwdriver was. The husband continued to deny it. Fed up, the judge eventually ruled this way, "If the husband has it, give it back." Yet again, the husband said he didn't have it, so that was that. We spent $5,000 on this issue, and they were in the exact same place they were when they started.

Be flexible. And don't spend $5,000 trying to track down a screwdriver.

Never use your children to get even with your ex-spouse.

Children need to feel loved and approved by both parents. They need to believe their parents can act in their best interests, and they do not need to constantly watch over their shoulders for any fighting.

No matter how angry, disappointed, and disgusted you might be by your child's other parent, it is in your child's best interest to keep that to yourself. Remember that your children are made up of 50 percent of each of their parents and anything disparaging you say about their other parent will be interpreted as a flaw in themselves. Be aware that your children are like sponges. They absorb feelings and words very easily.

And remember to always keep an eye on what's important to your child. I've heard parents grumble about having to take their sons or daughters to extracurricular activities that the other spouse encourages. They complain that after-school activities such as piano lessons or football practice cut into *their* time. But what they fail to see is it's not *their* time, it's their child's time. Put your kids first.

Be prepared for your deposition.

A deposition is a tool used by attorneys in a legal proceeding. They ask you questions while you are under oath, outside of court. Attorneys use these depositions to obtain additional information from the opposing party and assess that person's ability to handle difficult questions. There are some very simple ground rules to follow when you are having your deposition taken, which I have found to be extremely helpful.

1. Listen very carefully to the question asked and answer only that question.

2. Do not volunteer information. Despite your best intentions, attempting to expand your answer is never a good idea.

3. Make sure you understand the question before answering. Don't be afraid to ask for clarification.

4. If you do not know the answer, say so. Just because you are asked a question doesn't mean you must have an answer.

5. Do not bring any documents to the deposition unless advised to do so by your attorney.

6. If you are presented with documents during the deposition, take the time to review them before answering any questions about their contents.

7. Be polite and never become angry; anger will cloud your judgment when answering questions.

8. Do not hesitate to correct errors you may have made during the deposition.

9. **TELL THE TRUTH.** The absolute worst thing you can do in a deposition, or any other time you are under oath, is be dishonest. No matter how good of a liar you think you are, it will come back to bite you in the end. Just ask former President Bill Clinton.

Be sure your attorney prepares you for the deposition. This will usually consist of a one- to two-hour meeting with the attorney. During that meeting, the attorney should give you an idea of what he or she anticipates will be asked during the deposition.

I find it is very helpful to set up a mock deposition with the client. I will play the role of the opposing attorney, and I will have one of my associates represent our client. I'll then ask some easy questions to let my client get his or her feet wet and then slowly make the questions more and more difficult and annoying. This gives the clients a good idea of what to expect from an opposing attorney and themselves during the deposition.

When the deposition is complete, you will be given the opportunity to review the deposition transcript for the purpose of determining if the court reporter made an accurate recording of the questions as well as your answers. Do not ever waive the right to review the transcript. Despite their best efforts, court reporters have been known to make mistakes.

When I first began practicing, I heard of a story about an attorney who had the reputation for being one of the biggest jerks in town. In fact, he was proud of it. On one occasion, this attorney was taking the deposition of the opposing party, a sixty-seven-year-old former doctor. Midway through the deposition, the questions became more and more offensive, probing into areas of infidelity and hiding of assets. Suddenly, the deponent became flush and slumped over in his chair; he was having a heart attack. As the paramedics carted him away, this attorney shouted, "You're not going to get off that easily. I'm not done with your deposition."

Do not sign anything.

At least not before discussing it with your attorney. I have been involved with several cases wherein the two divorcing parties will get together and try to come up with an agreement. Always remember, there are legal ramifications to the agreements you may be signing and you should always discuss these things with your attorney first.

Don't rule out settling.

Keep in mind that the best option might be to settle your case at any time along the way. Even though you may have already spent $20,000 in attorney's fees, it may not be worth it to see the trial through to its completion. Always be willing to reassess your position. Is it really worth it to spend another $10,000 in fees just because you don't want to quit?

XI

Final Thoughts

Divorce can be painful. Divorce can be frustrating. But it can also be an opportunity for growth, understanding, and closure. Yes, the process can seem to drag on forever, but always keep in mind that eventually it'll be behind you. And, along the way, it will have opened a door to a remarkable new chapter in your life.

While the idea of preparing for your divorce while happily married may seem to be offensive and contrary to the very vows we take as husband and wife, my experience tells me that those individuals going through a divorce would have been much better off financially and emotionally if they had prepared better.

Going through a divorce impacts every aspect of one's life. Your attorney should be dedicated to making this transition as smooth as possible. He or she should have a network of professionals in other areas that can be utilized in an effort to make the process less intimidating. Your attorney should be willing to help you get in touch with a financial planner who can help prepare monthly budgets and strategies for saving assets, or help you find an accountant and an insurance agent who can assist you with tax planning and insuring that personal property and future child support and spousal maintenance obligations are secured. If necessary, your attorney should help you find an adult, or child, therapist to help you, or your children, cope with the emotional aspects of your divorce.

All of these professionals are part of my team approach to handling a family law matter. I strongly believe the job of a family law attorney is not only to provide clients with expert legal advice, but also to provide them with the tools necessary in order to move onto the next stage of their life. In order to do that, clients must be prepared.

After reading this book, you're well on your way.

GROUNDS FOR DIVORCE AND RESIDENCY REQUIREMENTS

State	No Fault Sole Ground	No Fault Added To Traditional	Incompatibility	Residency Requirements
Alabama		X	X	6 months
Alaska	X	X	X	6 months
Arizona	X	X		90 days
Arkansas		X		60 days
California	X			6 months
Colorado	X			90 days
Connecticut		X		1 year
Delaware		X	X	6 months
D.C.	X			6 months
Florida	X			6 months
Georgia		X		6 months
Hawaii				6 months
Idaho		X		6 weeks
Illinois		X		90 days
Indiana			X	60 days
Iowa	X			1 year
Kansas			X	60 days
Kentucky	X			180 days
Louisiana		X		6 months
Maine		X		6 months
Maryland		X		1 year
Massachusetts		X		None
Michigan	X			6 months

State	No Fault Sole Ground	No Fault Added To Traditional	Incompatibility	Residency Requirements
Minnesota	X			180 days
Mississippi		X		6 months
Missouri		X		90 days
Montana	X		X	90 days
Nebraska	X			1 year
Nevada			X	6 weeks
New Hampshire		X		1 year
New Jersey		X		1 year
New Mexico		X	X	6 months
New York		X		1 year
North Carolina		X		6 months
North Dakota		X		6 months
Ohio		X	X	6 months
Oklahoma			X	6 months
Oregon	X			6 months
Pennsylvania		X		6 months
Rhode Island		X		1 year
South Carolina		X		3 months (both residents)
South Dakota		X		None
Tennessee		X		6 months
Texas		X		6 months
Utah		X		90 days
Vermont		X		6 months
Virginia		X		6 months
Washington	X			1 year
West Virginia		X		1 year
Wisconsin	X			6 months
Wyoming		X	X	60 days

Appendix
B

1. *The Co-Parenting Survival Guide. Letting Go of Conflict After a Difficult Divorce.* Elizabeth S. Thayer, Ph.D. & Jeffrey Zimmerman, Ph.D.

2. *Mom's House, Dad's House, Making Two Homes for Your Child.* Isolina Ricci, Ph.D.

3. *Parents are Forever. A Step-by-Step Guide to Becoming Successful Coparents After Divorce.* Shirley Thomas, Ph.D.

4. *Making Divorce Easier on Your Child: 50 Ways to Help Children Adjust.* Nicholas Long, Ph.D. & Rex Forehand, Ph.D.

Appendix C

CUSTODY CRITERIA

State	Statutory Guidelines	Children's Wishes	Joint Custody
Alabama	X	X	X
Alaska	X	X	X
Arizona	X	X	X
Arkansas			
California	X	X	
Colorado	X	X	X
Connecticut		X	X
Delaware	X	X	X
D.C.	X	X	X
Florida	X	X	X
Georgia	X	X	X
Hawaii	X	X	X
Idaho	X	X	X
Illinois	X	X	X
Indiana	X	X	X
Iowa	X	X	X
Kansas	X	X	X
Kentucky	X	X	X
Louisiana	X	X	X
Maine	X	X	X
Maryland		X	X
Massachusetts			X
Michigan	X	X	X

State	Statutory Guidelines	Children's Wishes	Joint Custody
Minnesota	X	X	X
Mississippi	X		X
Missouri	X	X	X
Montana	X	X	X
Nebraska	X	X	X
Nevada	X	X	X
New Hampshire	X	X	X
New Jersey	X	X	X
New Mexico	X	X	X
New York		X	
North Carolina		X	X
North Dakota	X	X	X
Ohio	X	X	X
Oklahoma	X	X	X
Oregon	X	X	X
Pennsylvania	X	X	X
Rhode Island		X	X
South Carolina		X	X
South Dakota		X	X
Tennessee	X	X	X
Texas	X	X	X
Utah	X	X	X
Vermont	X	X	X
Virginia	X	X	X
Washington	X	X	
West Virginia	X	X	X
Wisconsin	X	X	X
Wyoming	X	X	X

STATE BY STATE (and District of Columbia) LIST FOR TAPE RECORDING TELEPHONE CALLS

A "one-party" state means at least one party to the telephone conversation has to have knowledge and give consent. In a "two-party" state, all parties must have knowledge and give consent.

State	One-party	Two-party
Alabama	X	
Alaska	X	
Arizona	X	
Arkansas	X	
California		X
Colorado	X	
Connecticut		X
Delaware		X
D.C.	X	
Florida		X
Georgia	X	
Hawaii	X	
Idaho	X	
Illinois	X	
Indiana	X	
Iowa	X	
Kansas	X	
Kentucky	X	
Louisiana	X	
Maine	X	

State	One-party	Two-party
Maryland		X
Massachusetts		X
Michigan	X	
Minnesota	X	
Mississippi	X	
Missouri	X	
Montana		X
Nebraska	X	
Nevada	X	
New Hampshire		X
New Jersey	X	
New Mexico	X	
New York	X	
North Carolina	X	
North Dakota	X	
Ohio	X	
Oklahoma	X	
Oregon	X	
Pennsylvania		X
Rhode Island	X	
South Carolina	X	
South Dakota	X	
Tennessee	X	
Texas	X	
Utah	X	
Vermont	X	
Virginia	X	
Washington		X
West Virginia	X	
Wisconsin	X	
Wyoming	X	

Appendix

E

CHILD SUPPORT GUIDELINES

State	Income Share	Percent of Income	College Support	Shared Parenting Time Offset
Alabama	X	X	X	
Alaska		X	X	X
Arizona	X			
Arkansas		X		
California	X			X
Colorado	X			X
Connecticut	X		X	
Delaware				X
D.C.		X	X	X
Florida	X			
Georgia		X		
Hawaii	X	X	X	X
Idaho	X			X
Illinois		X	X	
Indiana	X		X	X
Iowa		X	X	X
Kansas	X			X
Kentucky	X			
Louisiana	X			
Maine	X			
Maryland	X			X
Massachusetts		X	X	
Michigan	X		X	X
Minnesota		X^1		
Mississippi		X		

State	Income Share	Percent of Income	College Support	Shared Parenting Time Offset
Missouri	X		X	X
Montana				
Nebraska	X			X
Nevada		X		X
New Hampshire		X	X	
New Jersey	X		X	X
New Mexico	X			X
New York	X		X	
North Carolina	X			X
North Dakota		X		
Ohio	X			X
Oklahoma	X			X
Oregon	X		X	X
Pennsylvania	X			
Rhode Island	X			
South Carolina	X		X	
South Dakota	X			
Tennessee		X	X	X
Texas		X		
Utah	X			X
Vermont	X			X
Virginia	X			X
Washington	X		X	
West Virginia	X			X
Wisconsin		X		
Wyoming	X			X

1. Effective January 1, 2007, Minnesota will be using an Income Shares Approach.

F

PARENTAL ABDUCTION INFORMATION

If your child is abducted by your soon-to-be ex-spouse, these are some of the agencies you can call:

National Center for Missing and Exploited Children (NCMEC), 1-800-843-5678. Parents who fear abduction, or whose children have been abducted, should call the National Center as soon as possible.

State Missing Children's Clearinghouses. Many states have established missing children's clearinghouses to assist in the location, recovery, and return of missing and parentally-abducted children. Contact the National Center for Missing and Exploited Children, 1-800-843-5678, for the telephone number of the clearinghouse in your state.

Parent Locator Service. The State Parent Locator Service may be contacted for information and guidance on using the Federal Parent Locator Service to locate an abducting parent and abducted child. The locator service typically is part of the Office of Child Support Enforcement. The Federal Parent Locator Service may be contacted at (202) 401-9267.

Department of State: International Child Abductions. The U.S. Department of State has a Children's Issues Division in Washington, DC. The telephone number is (202) 647-2688.

The U.S. Central Authority under the Hague Convention on the Civil Aspects of International Child Abduction may be contacted at the same telephone number.

To prevent issuance of passports, contact the Office of Passport Services, which can be reached at (202) 955-0337, or fax the office at (202) 955-0230.

Department of Defense Worldwide Locator Services.

- Army Legal Assistance Division, Office of Judge Advocate General, (703) 697-3170.

- Navy Chief of Naval Personnel, (703) 614-2792.

- Marine Corps Head Legal Assistance Office, Judge Advocate Division, (703) 614-1513.

- Air Force AFLSA/JAJM, (202) 767-1539.

American Prosecutor Research Institute (APRI). Prosecution and Investigation of Parental Child Abduction Cases project, (703) 739-0321. APRI can provide information on parental abduction crimes and prosecutions to local prosecutors, which may (or may not) result in the filing of criminal charges against a perpetrator-parent.

INTERPOL, U.S. National Central Bureau (USNCB). (202) 616-9000. INTERPOL provides a global communications network to enable police around the world to coordinate international criminal investigations. In the U.S., the responsibility for missing persons and parental kidnapping cases lies with the Alien/Fugitive Enforcement Division.

American Bar Association Center on Children and the Law. (202) 662-1720; www.abanet.org/child.

About the Author

Jonathan J. Fogel, Esq. is an attorney practicing exclusively in the area of family law and is the owner of his own law firm, Fogel Law Offices, P.A. He has extensive experience handling divorces involving complex marital estates, spousal maintenance, custody disputes, and post decree matters.

He is a guest on many radio and television programs and is frequently asked to speak at seminars for continuing legal education and community groups. Jonathan shares his expertise with fellow attorneys as the chief author and editor of the publication *The Family Law Quarterly*. He also volunteers a great amount of his time representing indigent clients and working with battered women's shelters.

Jonathan lives in Minneapolis, Minnesota, with his *first* wife, Robin, and their three children, Noah, Sarah, and Isaac.